Linen, Wool, Cotton Kids

Linen, Wool, Cotton Kids

21 Patterns for Simple Separates and Comfortable Layers

Akiko Mano

ROOST BOOKS

Boston & London

2014

Contents

Introduction

I first started making children's clothes quite a long time ago, and my intention has always been to create kids' clothes that were smaller versions of adult clothing. I adore clothing that is lovely yet classic and that allows the nature of the fabric to come through.

In this book, in addition to the usual patterns, I tried to create more stylish coordinated separates that I hope you will enjoy. Worn on their own, each piece freely expresses the subtle character of its color or design. Choose basic colors and versatile fabrics for different seasons to make these separates interchangeable.

From feminine dresses to menswear-inspired outfits, girls have an inexplicable talent for wearing any clothing with flair. I hope that you'll make as many of these pieces as you like and that whichever lovely patterns you choose will capture that ineffable girlishness.

Akiko Mano

Spring and Summer

Create an array of outfits for your child by
mixing these spring and summer separates with
other clothes from your child's wardrobe.

E+R   F+N   J+I

E + C   D + N   J + H + K

A *Balloon Dress*

The gentle pouf of the hemline sways, catching
the air with every move. Choose a lightweight
fabric since the dress is sewn with double layers.

how to make … p. 42

B *Dual-Yoke Dress*

The artistic design of the yoke gives a subtly different effect from front to back, with the neckline rounded in front and V-shaped in the back. I created a silhouette with just the right amount of flare at the hemline.

how to make … p. 45

C *Jodhpur-Style Pants*

The elastic drawstring at the waist makes these
pants easy to wear. They are designed to be wear-
able in all seasons, so select the color and material
with this in mind.

how to make … p. 48

D *Button-Back Puffed-Sleeve Blouse*

The puffed sleeves on this blouse are a standard that always suits little girls, but with attention to details like the material and the opening at the back of the collar, the look is quite grown-up.

how to make … p. 51

E Ribbon-Back Tunic

The emphasis of this tunic is on the design
of its back. Adding gathers to the panel at the
low waist gives a soft and billowy effect.

how to make … p. 53

F Sleeveless Blouse

This is a variation on the Ribbon-Back
Tunic. A sheer fabric makes it feel light
and airy. Pair it with a camisole.

how to make … p. 56

G *Ribbon-Embellished Dress*

I adorned the square neckline with antique ribbon from my stash. Buttons in the back make for easy on, easy off.

how to make … p. 58

H *Stand-Collar Shirt*

Great for layering, this versatile piece works best in
a simple color. And since it's seamed up the center
front, the shirt is surprisingly easy to sew.

how to make … p. 61

I *Button-Back Tunic*

This shirt-style tunic has a collar and a sweet tuck in the center front. I chose this length because it's so fun to layer—it looks darling over a skirt or pants.

how to make … p. 64

J *Collared Vest*

This shawl-collared vest reminds me of old
menswear. Details like the buckle and welt
pockets make it even more authentic.

how to make … p. 67

Autumn and Winter

Autumn and winter clothes are such fun to layer.
Wear a jacket over a dress, or add a vest and a
jacket over a shirt, or even layer a dress over
another dress. Make as many separates in as many
versions as you like.

O+C   S+H+K   T+N

O+B   S+Q   T+R

21

K *Suspender Pants*

I was inspired by old European films to create these menswear suspender pants. The loose-fitting waist can be adjusted with the buckle in the back. The length of the suspenders can also be adjusted, so they can be used for a long time.

how to make … p. 70

L Reversible Vest

The fact that this simple vest is reversible makes it ideal. In linen or cotton, it works in all seasons. This solid version is crisp and sharp.

how to make … p. 74

Turn it inside out, and the pinstripes give it a more casual vibe. Playing with different fabric combinations makes reversible clothing so much fun.

M *Hooded Poncho*

For whatever reason, a girl in a hood is just adorable. This piece really plays up its childlike charm. Don't be nervous about sewing the hood—it's surprisingly simple.

how to make … p. 77

N *Yoke Panel Skirt*

Tucking in whatever top is worn with this skirt really
accentuates the panel's design. I think this length is
just adorable for girls.

how to make … p. 79

O Coat Dress

Buttoned or unbuttoned—this piece can be worn as a
dress or as a coat. Depending on what it's coordinated
with, it can be dressed up or dressed down.

how to make … p. 81

P Fleece Hat

Warm and stretchy fleece is the perfect material for this hat with earflaps. It's a cinch to make; create as many as you like in all different colors.

how to make … p. 83

Q *Pullover Dress*

This pullover design is styled like a shirtdress.
Button it all the way up to emphasize the tiny collar.
The front yoke uses a contrasting fabric, so have fun
playing with the combination.

how to make … p. 85

R *Knickerbocker Puffed Pants*

These knee-length pants have a yoke panel at the
waist. They create a lovely voluminous shape.

how to make … p. 89

S *Elbow-Patch Jacket*

The elbow patches are like men's work wear, but the cropped length also goes well with a skirt.

how to make … p. 92

T *Sailor-Collar Pullover*

This sailor collar holds some vintage charm. The tucks in the front and back give the shape plenty of room, making it such a comfortable layer.

how to make ... p. 95

U *Hooded Scarf*

This humorous design combines a hood and scarf
into one piece. And it's all the warmer, wrapped
around her neck.

how to make … p. 98

Step-by-Step Instructions

Notes on Making the Projects

Choosing the Right Size

· The actual-size patterns in the back of the book offer four sizes: 4, 5, 6, 7.

· Check your child's measurements against the size chart below to choose the most appropriate size. The amount of ease or length of the garment may vary depending on the design. If you are still uncertain about sizing, please also refer to the instructions page for the garment's finished measurements.

How to Use the Actual-Size Patterns

· Copy the actual-size patterns onto pattern paper. Using pattern paper, or any paper that is transparent enough to see the lines underneath, copy the patterns that you need. The necessary patterns are listed on the instructions page.

· The actual-size patterns are offered in four sizes, so please be careful to copy the correct size. It may be helpful to trace the size you need with a marker first.

· In addition to the finished garment lines, don't forget to also copy all markings, including the facing lines, fabric grain line, position of the pocket, and so on.

Fabric Preparation

· Since cotton and linen may shrink when washed, it's best to prewash these fabrics before sewing in order to preshrink them. To prewash, soak the fabric in water for several hours. Hang to dry and, while still slightly damp, iron the fabric along the grain.

Regarding Cutting

· **The actual-size patterns do not include seam allowances.** When cutting your fabric, add the necessary seam allowances according to the cutting layout.

· The cutting layout shows the pattern for size 5. Since the pattern arrangement may vary depending on the size, place the patterns on your fabric to confirm they fit before cutting.

Sizes	4	5	6	7
Height	39⅜"	43⅜"	47¼"	51⅛"
Chest	21¼"	22⅞"	24½"	26"
Waist	19¼"	20"	20⅞"	22"
Hips	22½"	23⅝"	24⅞"	26¾"
Sleeve	13"	14⅛"	15¾"	17"
Head	20"	20"	20½"	20⅞"

Sewing Techniques

These tips cover a range of techniques used in these garments. Refer to these, as well as to the explanations on the instruction pages.

Making Bias Tape   Use bias tape for the finishing of necklines and armholes.

When cutting from the same fabric, mark an equal measure along the length and width and then draw a diagonal line, at a 45-degree angle, connecting the two. Measure the width of the strip, parallel to the diagonal line, and cut. If one strip is not long enough, sew on another strip as shown in the diagram.

How to Cut

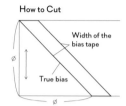

How to Sew Strips

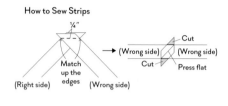

How to Hem   Use this double-fold, edge-stitched hem for finishing the fabric edge of hems and cuffs.

1
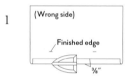

1. Fold the hem or cuff up by ⅜", and press.

2
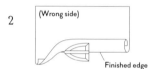

2. Fold the edge up again to create a double fold.

3

3. Stitch along the edge of the first fold.

Making a String Tie   It's easy to make a narrow string tie by neatly pressing the finished width and stitching.

1

1. Cut the fabric 4 times the width of the finished string tie.

2

2. Fold in half lengthwise, and press.

3

3. Open and fold each short end in by ⅜", and then fold each long side in to meet in the center.

4

4. Fold in half again along the original crease. Press flat.

5

5. Stitch along the edges.

Making Gathers   Here's the method for adding gathers using a sewing machine. If the gathered section is short, you may want to hand sew a running stitch instead of using a machine.

1
2

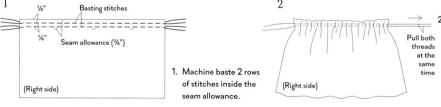

1. Machine baste 2 rows of stitches inside the seam allowance.

2. Pull both threads across the surface to make gathers. After sewing the piece to your garment, the basting stitches won't be visible on the right side so you may leave them or remove them as you prefer.

Making Patch Pockets How to sew perfectly tailored rounded pockets.

1
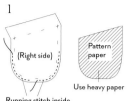

2

3
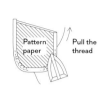

4
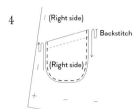

1. Using heavy (drawing) paper, make a pattern that is the size of the finished pocket. On the fabric for the pocket, hand sew a running stitch inside the seam allowance of the bottom curve.

2. Fold over the pocket's opening twice, and stitch.

3. Place the heavy pattern paper on the wrong side of the pocket. Press the fabric up over the paper around the seam allowance. Now pull the thread on the running stitches to tailor the curve.

4. Place the pocket in position on the garment, and machine stitch it in place. Backstitch securely at the beginning and end.

Attaching Sleeves Use these methods to sew standard set-in sleeves on jackets and blouses, as well as shirts with low sleeve caps.

Standard Set-in Sleeves

1

2
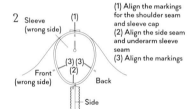

(1) Align the markings for the shoulder seam and sleeve cap
(2) Align the side seam and underarm sleeve seam
(3) Align the markings

3
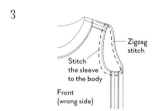

1. Sew the underarm sleeve seam, and finish the cuff. Prepare the body of the garment by sewing the shoulder and side seams.

2. Place the sleeve in the garment's armhole, right sides together. Pin it in place in the order shown in the diagram, then use smaller pins in between.

3. With the sleeve facing up, stitch it in place. If you have less experience, you may prefer to baste before stitching. Next, finish the seam allowances by binding them together with a zigzag stitch.

Sleeve Caps

1
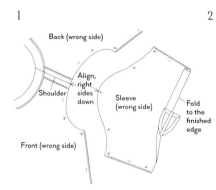

2
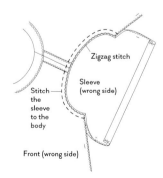

3
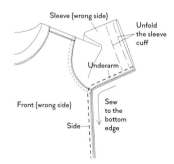

1. Sew the shoulder seam on the body, and prepare the sleeve edge by folding up the edge twice and pressing.

2. Place the sleeve along the body's armhole. Pin it in place with right sides together following the same order for the Standard Set-in Sleeves (see above) and stitch in place. Finish the seam allowances by binding them together with a zigzag stitch.

3. Place the front on the back, right sides together, and sew from the opening edge of the sleeve to the bottom hem.

A

Photograph
on page 8

Balloon Dress

Finished Measurements
(for sizes 4, 5, 6, and 7, respectively)

· Chest: 25¼", 26¾", 28⅜", 30"
· Dress length: 21¼", 23½", 25⅜", 27½"

Pattern Pieces: A from the Front of Sheet 1

· A Dress front (outer front, lining front)
· A Dress back (outer back, lining back)
· A Pocket
· A Pocket flap
For the loop, cut according to the measurements
shown on the cutting layout.

Materials
(for sizes 4, 5, 6, and 7, respectively)

· Cotton fabric (35"–36" wide): 2½ yards, 3 yards,
  3¼ yards, 3½ yards
· Button: (1) ⅜" diameter

Instructions
(★: Refer to the diagram)

1. Make the button loop, and baste it on. ★
2. Place the dress front on the dress back, right sides
   together, and sew the sides. Press open the seam
   allowances. Repeat for the lining.

3. Make the pockets and pocket flaps, and attach to
   the dress where indicated. ★
4. Place the dress and lining right sides together.
   Stitch along the neckline and armholes, leaving
   the shoulders unsewn. Turn the dress right side
   out. ★
5. Sew the shoulder seams. First, place the
   shoulders of the dress front on the dress back,
   right sides together, and sew. Press open the seam
   allowances. Next, whipstitch the shoulders of the
   lining together. (See page 69.)
6. Topstitch along the neckline and armholes.
7. Add gathers to the hem of the dress (see page 40),
   pulling the threads and shaping the dress until
   the hem aligns with the hem of the lining. With
   wrong sides together, sew the hem of the dress to
   the lining.
8. Attach the button.

Cutting Layout (Size 5)

Right side of fabric

Add a seam allowance of ⅜"
unless otherwise specified.

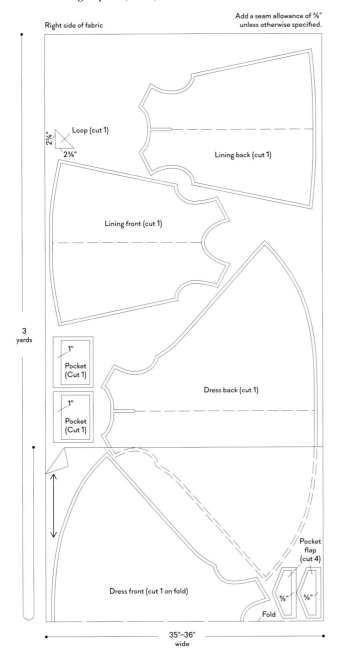

2⅜"

Loop (cut 1)

2⅜"

Lining back (cut 1)

Lining front (cut 1)

3
yards

1"
Pocket
(Cut 1)

1"
Pocket
(Cut 1)

Dress back (cut 1)

Pocket
flap
(cut 4)

⅝"   ⅝"

Dress front (cut 1 on fold)

Fold

35"–36"
wide

1. Make the button loop, and baste it on.

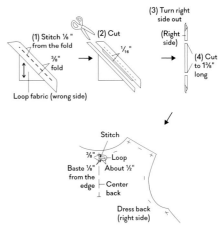

(1) Stitch ⅛"
from the fold

(2) Cut

¹⁄₁₆"

(3) Turn right
side out

(Right
side)

(4) Cut
to 1⅜"
long

⅜"
fold

Loop fabric (wrong side)

Stitch

⅜"

Loop

Baste ⅛"
from the
edge

About ½"

Center
back

Dress back
(right side)

Order of Instructions

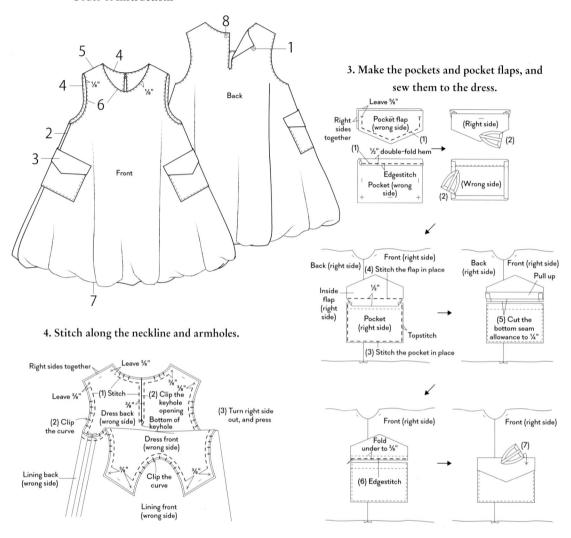

Back

Front

3. Make the pockets and pocket flaps, and sew them to the dress.

Leave ⅝"

Right sides together

Pocket flap (wrong side)

(1)

(Right side)

(2)

(1) ½" double-fold hem

Edgestitch

Pocket (wrong side)

(2)

(Wrong side)

(2)

Front (right side)

Back (right side)

(4) Stitch the flap in place

Inside flap (right side)

½"

Pocket (right side)

Topstitch

(3) Stitch the pocket in place

Back (right side)

Front (right side)

Pull up

(5) Cut the bottom seam allowance to ¼"

Front (right side)

Fold under to ⅜"

(6) Edgestitch

Front (right side)

(7)

4. Stitch along the neckline and armholes.

Right sides together

Leave ⅜"

⅜"

⅜"

Leave ⅜"

(1) Stitch

⅜"

(2) Clip the keyhole opening

Dress back (wrong side)

Bottom of keyhole

(3) Turn right side out, and press

(2) Clip the curve

Dress front (wrong side)

Lining back (wrong side)

⅜"

Clip the curve

⅜"

Lining front (wrong side)

7. Add gathers to the hem of the dress, and align it with the hem of the lining. Place wrong sides together, and sew the hems closed.

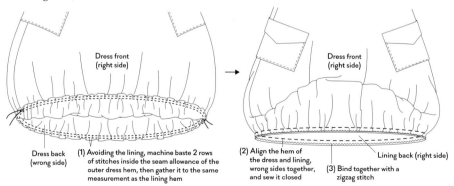

Dress front (right side)

Dress back (wrong side)

(1) Avoiding the lining, machine baste 2 rows of stitches inside the seam allowance of the outer dress hem, then gather it to the same measurement as the lining hem

Dress front (right side)

(2) Align the hem of the dress and lining, wrong sides together, and sew it closed

Lining back (right side)

(3) Bind together with a zigzag stitch

B

Back view

Photograph
on page 9

Dual-Yoke Dress

Finished Measurements
(for sizes 4, 5, 6, and 7, respectively)

· Chest: 40⅛", 41¾", 43⅜", 44⅞"
· Dress length: 23¼", 25¼", 27⅛", 29⅛"

Pattern Pieces: B from the Back of Sheet 1

· B Dress front
· B Dress back
· B Front yoke
· B Back yoke
· B Pocket

For the bias tape to finish the armholes, cut according to the measurements shown on the cutting layout.

Materials
(for sizes 4, 5, 6, and 7, respectively)

· Cotton/linen fabric (44"–45" wide): 1½ yards, 1½ yards, 1¾ yards, 1¾ yards
· Fusible interfacing: 36" x 15¾"

Preparation

· Apply fusible interfacing to the front and back yokes and to the seam allowance of the sides of the dress front where the pocket openings will be placed.
· Finish the edges of the dress sides and pockets with a zigzag stitch (or overlock stitch).

Instructions
(★: Refer to the diagram)

1. Finish the armholes with bias tape. ★
2. Add gathers to the dress front and back, and attach the front and back yokes. ★
3. Sew the side seams, and make the pockets. ★
4. Sew the shoulder seams of the yoke and yoke lining, respectively, and press open the seam allowances.
5. Sew the neckline. Place the yoke and yoke lining right sides together, and stitch around the neckline. Fold over the upper seam allowance of the yoke lining, and press. Turn the dress right side out, and topstitch around the neckline and bottom edge of the yoke to secure the yoke lining to the yoke. ★
6. Create a double-fold hem by folding the edge up ¼" then again by ¾", and stitch it in place.

Cutting Layout (Size 5)

Add a seam allowance of ⅜" unless otherwise specified.

⋯⋯ denotes where to apply interfacing

Right side of fabric

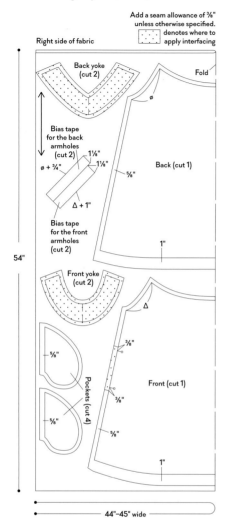

Back yoke (cut 2)

Fold

Bias tape for the back armholes (cut 2)

ø

1⅛"

1⅛"

ø + ¾"

Back (cut 1)

⅝"

Δ + 1"

Bias tape for the front armholes (cut 2)

1"

Front yoke (cut 2)

Δ

⅝"

⅝"

⅜"

Pockets (cut 4)

Front (cut 1)

⅜"

⅝"

1"

54"

44"–45" wide

Order of Instructions

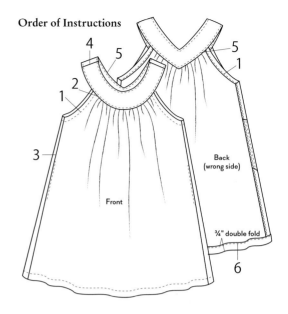

4

5

5

1

2

1

3

Back (wrong side)

Front

¾" double fold

6

1. Finish the armholes with bias tape.

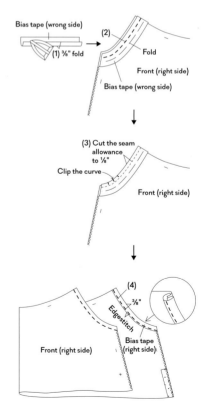

Bias tape (wrong side)

(1) ⅜" fold

(2)

Fold

Front (right side)

Bias tape (wrong side)

(3) Cut the seam allowance to ⅛"

Clip the curve

Front (right side)

(4)

⅜"

Edgestitch

Front (right side)

Bias tape (right side)

Finish the back armhole in the same way

2. Add gathers to the dress front and back, and attach the front and back yokes.

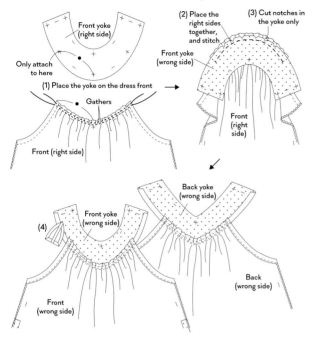

Front yoke (right side)

Only attach to here

(1) Place the yoke on the dress front

Gathers

Front (right side)

(2) Place the right sides together, and stitch

(3) Cut notches in the yoke only

Front yoke (wrong side)

Front (right side)

(4)

Front yoke (wrong side)

Back yoke (wrong side)

Front (wrong side)

Back (wrong side)

3. Sew the side seams, and make the pockets.

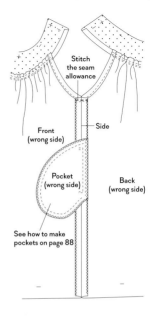

Stitch the seam allowance

Front (wrong side)

Side

Pocket (wrong side)

Back (wrong side)

See how to make pockets on page 88

5. Sew the neckline.

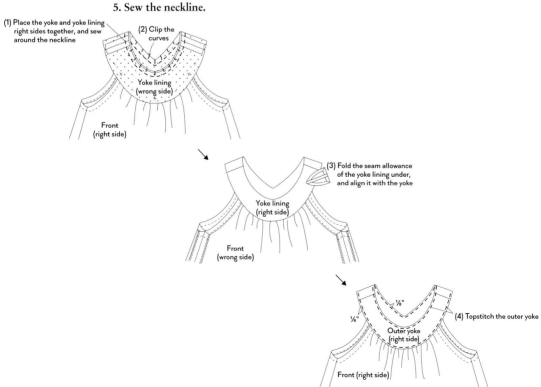

(1) Place the yoke and yoke lining right sides together, and sew around the neckline

(2) Clip the curves

Yoke lining (wrong side)

Front (right side)

(3) Fold the seam allowance of the yoke lining under, and align it with the yoke

Yoke lining (right side)

Front (wrong side)

⅛"

⅛"

(4) Topstitch the outer yoke

Outer yoke (right side)

Front (right side)

C

Photograph
on page 10

Jodhpur-Style Pants

Finished Measurements
(for sizes 4, 5, 6, and 7, respectively)

· Hips: 28", 29⅛", 30⅜", 32¼"
· Pant length: 17¾", 19⅝", 21¼", 22¾"

Pattern Pieces: C from the Front of Sheet 2

· C Pants front
· C Pants back
· C Front cuff
· C Back cuff

For the waistband and drawstring tie, cut according to the measurements shown on the cutting layout.

Materials
(for sizes 4, 5, 6, and 7, respectively)

· Linen fabric (35"–36" wide): 1¼ yards, 1¼ yards, 1½ yards, 1½ yards
· Fusible interfacing: 36" x 15¾"
· Buttons: (6) ⅜" diameter
· Elastic: ⅜" wide x 18", 19", 19¾", 20¾" long

Preparation

· Apply fusible interfacing to the cuffs.
· Finish the edges of the pants sides and inseams with a zigzag stitch (or overlock stitch).

Instructions
(★: Refer to the diagram)

1. Sew the side seams. Starting from the waist, sew to the top of the vent at the bottom of the pant leg. Press the seam allowance open, then stitch it in place. ★
2. Sew the inseams, and press open the seam allowances. ★
3. Add gathers to the hem, and attach the cuffs. ★
4. Sew the crotch. Finish the seam allowances by binding them together with a zigzag stitch. ★
5. Attach the waistband. Make buttonholes in the center of the waistband for the drawstring tie to pass through, then attach it to the waist of the pants. ★
6. Make the drawstring tie. Fold the tie into quarters to a width of ⅜", then stitch the edges. (See page 40.)
7. Insert the elastic and the drawstring tie through the waistband. Sew the ends of the elastic together with a ¾" overlap.
8. Make buttonholes on the front side of the cuff, and attach the buttons to the back placket.

Cutting Layout (Size 5)

Add a seam allowance of ⅜"
unless otherwise specified.

[⠿] denotes where to
apply interfacing

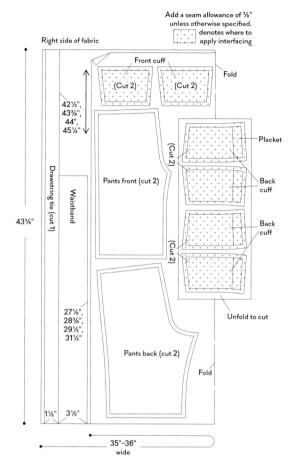

Right side of fabric

Front cuff

(Cut 2)   (Cut 2)   Fold

42½",
43⅜",
44",
45¼"

(Cut 2)

Placket

Pants front (cut 2)

Back cuff

Drawstring tie (cut 1)

Waistband

(Cut 2)

Back cuff

43⅜"

27⅛",
28⅜",
29½",
31½"

Unfold to cut

Pants back (cut 2)

Fold

1½"   3½"

35"–36"
wide

Order of Instructions

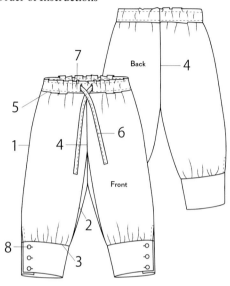

Back

Front

7
5
1
4
6
2
3
8
4

1. Sew the side seams.

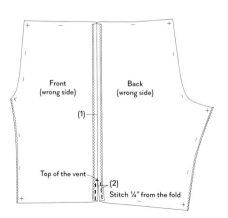

Front
(wrong side)

Back
(wrong side)

(1)

Top of the vent

(2)
Stitch ¼" from the fold

2. Sew the inseams.

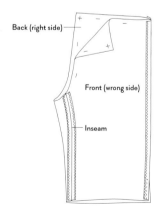

Back (right side)

Front (wrong side)

Inseam

3. Add gathers to the hem, and attach the cuffs.

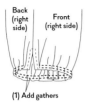

Back (right side)
Front (right side)

(1) Add gathers

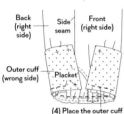

Outer back cuff (wrong side)
Outer front cuff (wrong side)
Interfacing side

(2) Sew the inseams

(3) Fold the seam allowance only on the inner cuffs

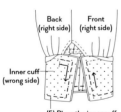

Inner front cuff (wrong side)
Inner back cuff (wrong side)

↓

Back (right side)
Side seam
Front (right side)

Outer cuff (wrong side)
Placket

(4) Place the outer cuff on the pant leg, right sides together, and sew

↓

Back (right side)
Front (right side)

Inner cuff (wrong side)

(5) Place the inner cuff on the outer cuff, right sides together, and sew

↓

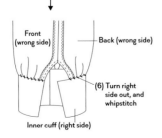

Front (wrong side)
Back (wrong side)

(6) Turn right side out, and whipstitch

Inner cuff (right side)

4. Sew the crotch.

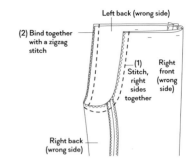

Left back (wrong side)

(2) Bind together with a zigzag stitch

(1) Stitch, right sides together

Right front (wrong side)

Right back (wrong side)

5. Attach the waistband.

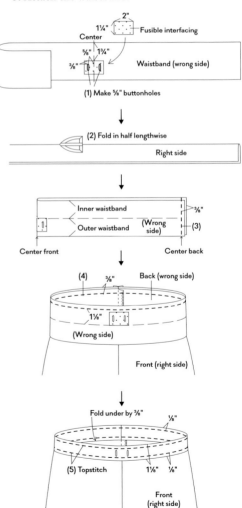

2"
1¼"
Center
⅝" 1¾"
⅜"
Fusible interfacing
Waistband (wrong side)

(1) Make ⅝" buttonholes

↓

(2) Fold in half lengthwise
Right side

↓

Inner waistband
Outer waistband (Wrong side)
⅜"
(3)

Center front
Center back

↓

(4) ⅜" Back (wrong side)

1⅛"

(Wrong side)

Front (right side)

↓

Fold under by ⅜" ⅛"

(5) Topstitch 1⅛" ⅛"

Front (right side)

D

Photograph
on page 11

Back view

Button-Back Puffed-Sleeve Blouse

Finished Measurements

(for sizes 4, 5, 6, and 7, respectively)

- Chest: 24⅜", 26", 27½", 29⅛"
- Length: 14½", 15¾", 17", 18⅛"
- Sleeve length: 6⅛", 6½", 6⅞", 7¼"

Pattern Pieces: D from the Front of Sheet 2

- D Blouse front
- D Blouse back
- D Collar
- D Sleeve

For the bias tape to finish the neckline, cut according to the measurements shown on the cutting layout.

Materials

(for sizes 4, 5, 6, and 7, respectively)

- Linen fabric (58"–60" wide): ¾ yard
- Fusible interfacing: 4" x 21⅝"
- Buttons: (5) ⅜" diameter
- Elastic: (2) ¼" wide x 7⅞", 8¼", 8⅝", 9" long

Preparation

- Apply fusible interfacing to the back facing.
- Finish the seam allowance of the shoulders, sides, underarms, and the back facing with a zigzag stitch (or overlock stitch).

Instructions

(★: Refer to the diagram)

1. Sew the shoulder seams, and press open the seam allowances.
2. Make the collar. (See page 66.)
3. Attach the collar. Baste the collar to the neckline of the blouse, then layer the bias tape and sew it in place. Finish the seam allowance by wrapping it with the bias tape. (See page 66.)
4. Sew the side seams, and press open the seam allowances.
5. Finish the hem. First, fold under the facings, and press. Create a double-fold hem by folding up the edge by ⅜" twice and stitching it in place, starting and stopping at the edge of the facing. (See page 40.)
6. Make the sleeves. When sewing the underarms, leave an opening in the seam allowance for inserting the elastic. ★
7. Attach the sleeves. Finish the seam allowances by binding them together with a zigzag stitch. (See page 41.)
8. Insert the elastic through the gap in the sleeve side seam. Sew the ends of the elastic together with a ¾" overlap.
9. Make the buttonholes, and attach the buttons. Make sure the buttonholes are vertical.

Cutting Layout (Size 5)

Add a seam allowance of ⅜"
unless otherwise specified.

[···] denotes where to apply interfacing

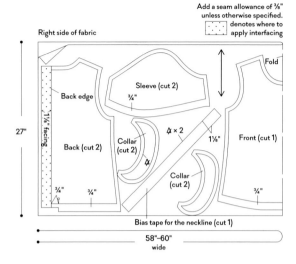

Right side of fabric

Fold

Sleeve (cut 2)
¾"

Back edge

1⅛" facing

27"

Back (cut 2)

Collar (cut 2)

4 × 2

1⅛"

Front (cut 1)

4

Collar (cut 2)

¾"   ¾"

¾"

Bias tape for the neckline (cut 1)

58"–60"
wide

Order of Instructions

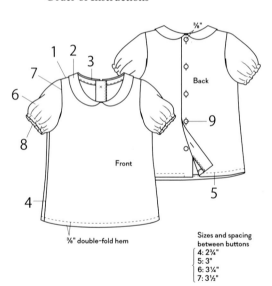

⅜"

Back

1 2
3

7

6

9

8

Front

5

4

⅜" double-fold hem

Sizes and spacing
between buttons
4: 2¾"
5: 3"
6: 3¼"
7: 3½"

6. Make the sleeves.

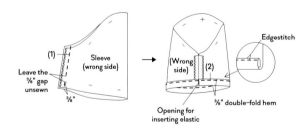

(1)

Sleeve
(wrong side)

Leave the
⅜" gap
unsewn

⅜"

(Wrong
side) (2)

Opening for
inserting elastic

⅜" double-fold hem

Edgestitch

E

Photograph
on page 12

Back view

Ribbon-Back Tunic

Finished Measurements
(for sizes 4, 5, 6, and 7, respectively)

· Chest: 25½", 27⅛", 28¾", 30⅜"
· Length: 16½", 18⅛", 19⅝", 21¼"

Pattern Pieces: E from the Front of Sheet 1

· E Blouse front
· E Blouse back
· E Skirt ruffle front and back
· E Frilled sleeve

For the facing for the front and back of the neckline, make your own pattern by copying the outline of the neckline, as shown on the cutting layout.

For the string tie and the bias tape to finish the armholes, cut according to the measurements shown on the cutting layout.

Materials
(for sizes 4, 5, 6, and 7, respectively)

· Cotton/linen fabric (58"–60" wide): ¾ yards, ¾ yards, 1 yard, 1 yard
· Fusible interfacing: 23⅝" x 6"

Preparation

· Apply fusible interfacing to the front and back neckline facing.
· Finish the seam allowances of the shoulders and sides of the blouse front and back and the skirt ruffle; secure the edges of the facing with a zigzag stitch (or overlock stitch).

Instructions
(★: Refer to diagram)

1. Sew together the shoulder seams of the blouse and the facing, respectively, and press open the seam allowances.
2. Make the frilled sleeves, and attach them to the blouse. Finish the seam allowances with the bias tape. ★
3. Make the string tie. Fold the tie into quarters, to a width of ⅜", then stitch the edges. (See page 40.)
4. With the facing in place, backstitch the neckline and finish the back closure. At the same time, fasten the string tie between the back edges of the facing. ★
5. Sew the side seams, and add gathers to the bottom edge of the blouse. ★
6. Sew the skirt ruffle. Sew the side seams, then create a double-fold hem by folding up the fabric edge by ⅜" twice and stitching it in place. Then add gathers along the upper edge. ★
7. Sew together the blouse and the skirt ruffle. Finish the seam allowances by binding them together with a zigzag stitch that lies against the blouse edge.

Cutting Layout (Size 5)

Add a seam allowance of ⅜"
unless otherwise specified.

:::: denotes where to
apply interfacing

Right side of fabric

Armhole bias tape
(cut 2)

Fold

Frilled sleeve

0"

¾"

Back neckline
facing (cut 2)

0"

¾"

Fold

● + △ + ¾"
1⅛"

Front neckline facing (cut 1)

27"

1½"

△

Back (cut 2)

15",
15¾",
16½",
17⅜"

Front (cut 1)

String tie (cut 2)

Skirt ruffle back (cut 1)

¾"

Skirt ruffle front (cut 1)

¾"

58"–60"
wide

Order of Instructions

3

1   4

2

4   Back

5   Front

7

6

2. Make the frilled sleeves, and attach them to the blouse.

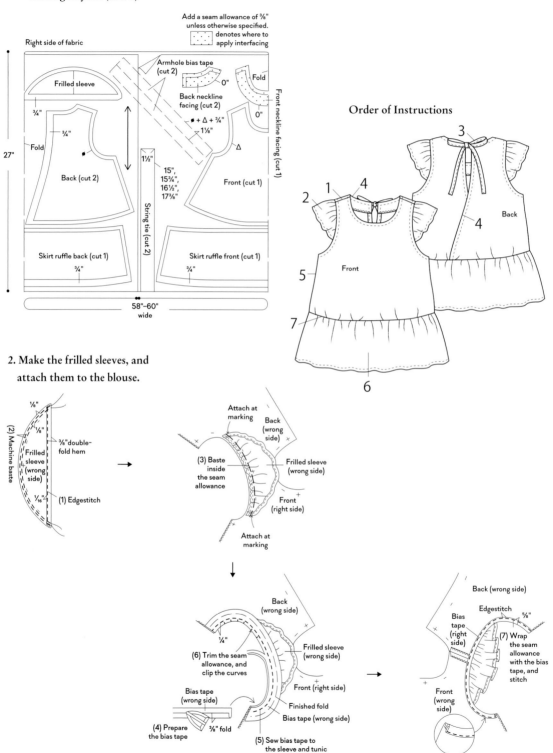

⅛"

⅛"

(2) Machine baste

¾" double-fold hem

Frilled sleeve (wrong side)

1/16"   (1) Edgestitch

Attach at marking

Back (wrong side)

(3) Baste inside the seam allowance

Frilled sleeve (wrong side)

Front (right side)

Attach at marking

Back (wrong side)

¼"

(6) Trim the seam allowance, and clip the curves

Frilled sleeve (wrong side)

Front (right side)

Bias tape (wrong side)

(4) Prepare the bias tape

⅜" fold

Finished fold

Bias tape (wrong side)

(5) Sew bias tape to the sleeve and tunic along the fold

Back (wrong side)

Edgestitch   ⅝"

Bias tape (right side)

(7) Wrap the seam allowance with the bias tape, and stitch

Front (wrong side)

54

4. With the facing in place, backstitch the neckline and finish the back closure.

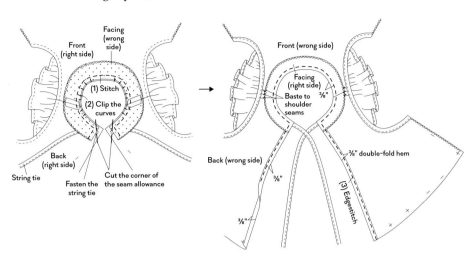

5. Sew the side seams, and add gathers to the bottom edge of the blouse.

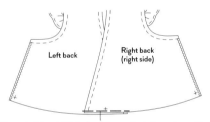

(1) Layer the left and right backs so they overlap in the center, and baste.

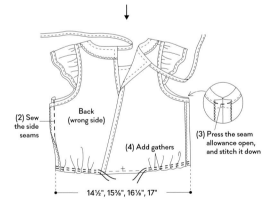

6. Sew the skirt ruffle.

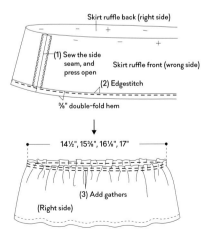

F

Photograph
on page 12

Back view

Sleeveless Blouse

Finished Measurements
(for sizes 4, 5, 6, and 7, respectively)

· Chest: 25½", 27⅛", 28¾", 30⅜"
· Length: 13⅛", 14⅜", 15½", 16¾"

Pattern Pieces: F from the Front of Sheet 1

· F Blouse front
· F Blouse back
· F Bottom band

For the facing for the front and back of the neckline, make your own pattern by copying the outline of the neckline, as shown on the cutting layout.

For the string tie and the bias tape to finish the armholes, cut according to the measurements shown on the cutting layout.

Materials
(for sizes 4, 5, 6, and 7)

· Cotton/linen fabric (58"–60" wide): ¾ yards
· Fusible interfacing: 23⅝" x 6"

Preparation

· Apply fusible interfacing to the front and back neckline facing.
· Finish the seam allowances of the shoulders and sides and the edges of the facing with a zigzag stitch (or overlock stitch).

Instructions
(★: Refer to diagram)

1. Sew together the shoulder seams of the blouse and the facing, respectively, and press open the seam allowances.
2. Finish the armholes with the bias tape. (See page 46.)
3. Make the string tie. Fold the tie into quarters, to a width of ⅜", then stitch the edges. (See page 40.)
4. With the facing in place, backstitch the neckline and finish the back closure. At the same time, fasten the string tie between the back closure of the facing. (See page 55.)
5. Sew the side seams, and add gathers to the bottom edge of the blouse. (See page 55.)
6. Sew the bottom band, and attach it to the bottom edge of the blouse. Finish the seam allowances by binding them together with a zigzag stitch that lies against the blouse edge. ★

Cutting Layout (Size 5)

Add a seam allowance of ⅜"
unless otherwise specified.
⠿ denotes where to
apply interfacing

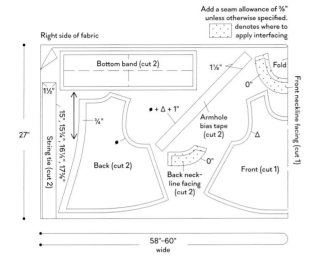

Right side of fabric

Bottom band (cut 2)

1⅛"

0"

Fold

Front neckline facing (cut 1)

1½"

15", 15¾", 16½", 17⅞"

¾"

⊙ + △ + 1"

Armhole
bias tape
(cut 2)

String tie (cut 2)

△

Back (cut 2)

0"

Front (cut 1)

Back neck-
line facing
(cut 2)

27"

58"–60"
wide

Order of Instructions

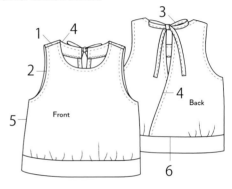

1
4
3

2

5

Front

4

Back

6

6. Sew the bottom band, and attach it to the bottom edge of the blouse.

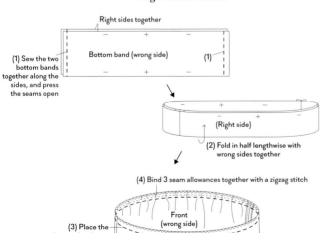

Right sides together

Bottom band (wrong side)

(1)

(1) Sew the two
bottom bands
together along the
sides, and press
the seams open

(Right side)

(2) Fold in half lengthwise with
wrong sides together

(4) Bind 3 seam allowances together with a zigzag stitch

Front
(wrong side)

(3) Place the
bottom band over
right side of blouse,
and sew it in place

Fold

Bottom band

Back
(right side)

G

Photograph
on page 14

Ribbon-Embellished Dress

Finished Measurements

(for sizes 4, 5, 6, and 7, respectively)

· Chest: 41", 42½", 44", 45⅝"
· Length (from shoulder): 22", 24", 26", 28"

Pattern Pieces: G from the Front of Sheet 2

· G Dress front
· G Dress back
· G Front center yoke
· G Front shoulder yoke
· G Back center yoke
· G Back shoulder yoke
· G Sleeve
· G Pocket

To make the placket facing for the back opening, cut according to the measurements shown on the cutting layout.

Materials

(for sizes 4, 5, 6, and 7, respectively)

· Linen fabric (58"–60" wide): 1 yard, 1 yard, 1 yard, 1¼ yards
· Ribbon: 2" x 2 yards
· Buttons: (2) ½" diameter

A Note about Cutting

· All the pieces for the yoke are cut from the ribbon.

Preparation

· Finish the seam allowances of the shoulders, sides, and underarms with a zigzag stitch (or overlock stitch).

Instructions

(★: Refer to diagram)

1. Make and attach the pockets. (See page 41.)
2. Make the opening at the back center. ★
3. Add gathers to the dress, and sew the ribbon yoke. ★
4. Sew the shoulder seams, and press open the seam allowances.
5. Sew the ribbon to make the inner yoke. ★
6. Sew the back edges of the inner and outer yokes, and the neckline. ★
7. Attach the sleeves. Finish the seam allowances by binding them together with a zigzag stitch. (See page 41.)
8. Sew along the underarm sleeve and side seams. Press open the seam allowances.
9. Fold the arm cuff up by ⅜" and again by ⅝" to create a double-fold hem. Stitch it in place.
10. Fold the hem up by ⅜" and again by ¾" to create a double-fold hem. Stitch it in place.
11. Using thread, make 2 chain-stitch thread loops on the edge of the right back yoke; attach the buttons to the left back yoke. You may also use a bulkier thread for the loops. ★

Cutting Layout (Size 5)

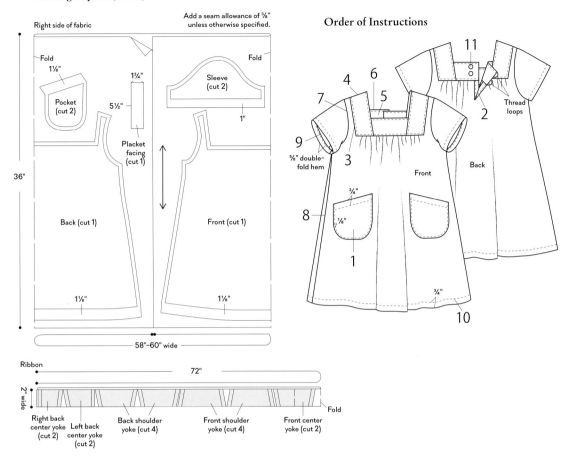

Add a seam allowance of ⅜" unless otherwise specified.

Right side of fabric

Fold

1⅛"

Pocket (cut 2)

1¾"

5½"

Sleeve (cut 2)

Fold

1"

Placket facing (cut 1)

36"

Back (cut 1)

Front (cut 1)

1⅛"

1⅛"

58"–60" wide

Ribbon

72"

2" wide

Fold

Right back center yoke (cut 2)

Left back center yoke (cut 2)

Back shoulder yoke (cut 4)

Front shoulder yoke (cut 4)

Front center yoke (cut 2)

Order of Instructions

11

4 6 5

7

2

Thread loops

9

⅝" double-fold hem

3

Front

Back

8

¾"

⅛"

1

¾"

10

2. Make the opening at the back center.

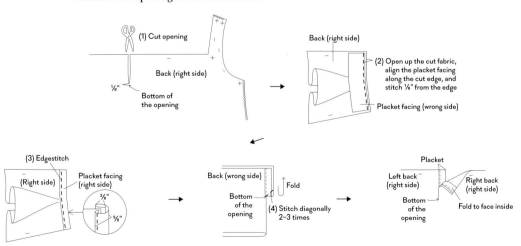

(1) Cut opening

Back (right side)

⅛"

Bottom of the opening

Back (right side)

(2) Open up the cut fabric, align the placket facing along the cut edge, and stitch ⅛" from the edge

Placket facing (wrong side)

(3) Edgestitch

(Right side)

Placket facing (right side)

⅜"

⅝"

Back (wrong side)

Fold

Bottom of the opening

(4) Stitch diagonally 2–3 times

Placket

Left back (right side)

Right back (right side)

Bottom of the opening

Fold to face inside

3. Add gathers to the dress, and sew the ribbon yoke.

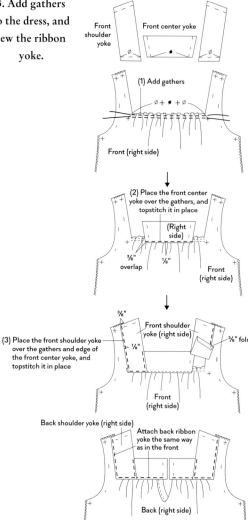

Front shoulder yoke

Front center yoke

(1) Add gathers

⌀ + ● + ⌀

Front (right side)

(2) Place the front center yoke over the gathers, and topstitch it in place

(Right side)

³⁄₈" overlap   ¹⁄₈"

Front (right side)

³⁄₈"

(3) Place the front shoulder yoke over the gathers and edge of the front center yoke, and topstitch it in place

Front shoulder yoke (right side)

¹⁄₈"   ³⁄₈" fold

Front (right side)

Back shoulder yoke (right side)

Attach back ribbon yoke the same way as in the front

Back (right side)

11. Make the thread loops.

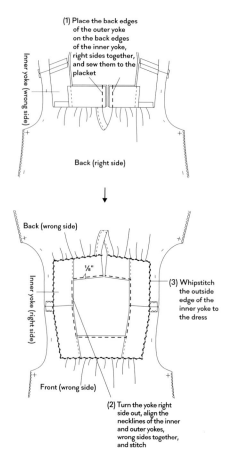

Inner right back yoke

Back edge

Back edge

Pull the thread through and make a chain.

³⁄₈"

Catch and secure   ³⁄₈"

5. Sew the ribbon to make the inner yoke.

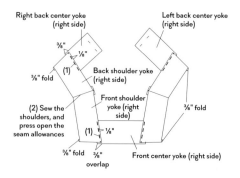

Right back center yoke (right side)

Left back center yoke (right side)

³⁄₈" fold

³⁄₈" fold

¹⁄₈"

(1)

³⁄₈" fold

Back shoulder yoke (right side)

Front shoulder yoke (right side)

³⁄₈" fold

(2) Sew the shoulders, and press open the seam allowances

(1)   ¹⁄₈"

³⁄₈" fold   ³⁄₈" overlap

Front center yoke (right side)

6. Sew the back edges of the inner and outer yokes, and the neckline.

(1) Place the back edges of the outer yoke on the back edges of the inner yoke, right sides together, and sew them to the placket

Inner yoke (wrong side)

Back (right side)

Back (wrong side)

Inner yoke (right side)

¹⁄₈"

(3) Whipstitch the outside edge of the inner yoke to the dress

Front (wrong side)

(2) Turn the yoke right side out, align the necklines of the inner and outer yokes, wrong sides together, and stitch

H

Photograph
on page 15

Stand-Collar Shirt

Finished Measurements

(for sizes 4, 5, 6, and 7, respectively)

· Chest: 27½", 29⅛", 30¾", 32¼"
· Length: 15⅜", 16¾", 18⅛", 19½"
· Sleeve length: 5⅛", 5½", 6⅛", 6½"

Pattern Pieces: H from the Back of Sheet 2

· H Front
· H Back
· H Collar
· H Sleeve
· H Trim

Materials

(for sizes 4, 5, 6, and 7)

· Linen fabric (58"–60" wide): ¾ yards

Preparation

· Finish the seam allowances of the shoulders, sides, and underarms with a zigzag stitch (or overlock stitch).

Instructions

(★: Refer to diagram)

1. Sew the center-back tuck. ★
2. Sew the center front. Create a double-fold hem with the seam allowance, and make 4 rows of stitches on the right and on the left. ★
3. Attach the trim at the bottom of the front opening. ★
4. Sew the shoulders, and press open the seam allowances.
5. Make the collar. ★
6. Attach the collar. Sew together the outer collar and the shirt, and with the seam allowance lying against the shirt edge, whipstitch the inner collar. (See page 97.)
7. Add gathers to the sleeves, and attach them to the shirt. Stitch the seam allowance so that it lies against the shirt edge. ★
8. Sew along the underarm sleeve and side seams. Press open the seam allowances. ★
9. Create a double-fold hem at the sleeve edges by folding the fabric edge up by ½" twice and stitching it in place.
10. Create a double-fold hem at the shirt edge by folding the fabric edge up by ¼" twice and stitching it in place.

Cutting Layout (Size 5)

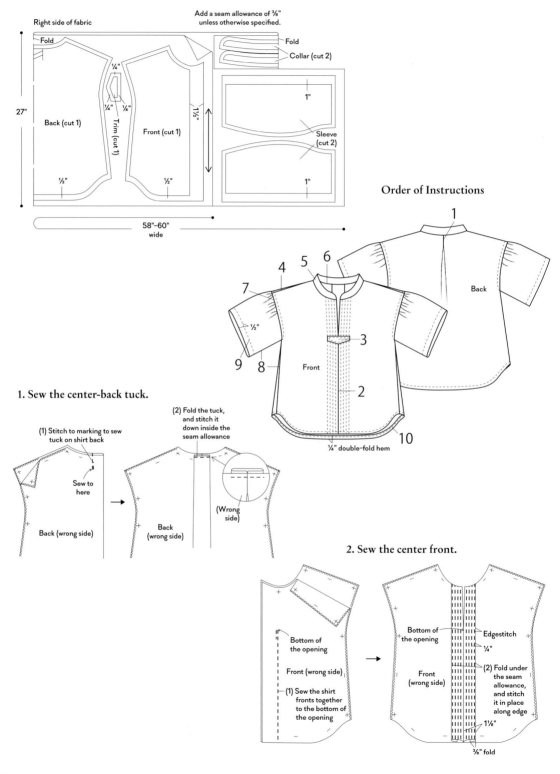

Add a seam allowance of ⅜"
unless otherwise specified.

Right side of fabric

Fold

Fold

Collar (cut 2)

¼"

¼"   ¼"

Trim (cut 1)

1½"

27"

Back (cut 1)

Front (cut 1)

1"

Sleeve
(cut 2)

½"

½"

1"

58"–60"
wide

Order of Instructions

1

Back

4   5   6

7

½"

9   8

Front

3

2

10

¼" double-fold hem

1. Sew the center-back tuck.

(1) Stitch to marking to sew
tuck on shirt back

(2) Fold the tuck,
and stitch it
down inside the
seam allowance

Sew to
here

Back (wrong side)

Back
(wrong side)

(Wrong
side)

2. Sew the center front.

Bottom of
the opening

Front (wrong side)

(1) Sew the shirt
fronts together
to the bottom of
the opening

Bottom of
the opening

Front
(wrong side)

Edgestitch

¼"

(2) Fold under
the seam
allowance,
and stitch
it in place
along edge

1⅛"

⅜" fold

3. Attach the trim at the bottom of the front opening.

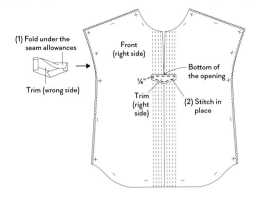

(1) Fold under the seam allowances

Trim (wrong side)

Front (right side)

Bottom of the opening

⅛"

Trim (right side)

(2) Stitch in place

5. Make the collar.

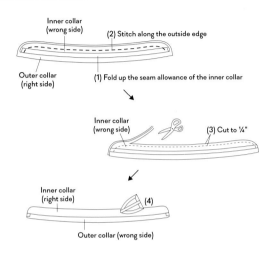

Inner collar (wrong side)

(2) Stitch along the outside edge

Outer collar (right side)

(1) Fold up the seam allowance of the inner collar

Inner collar (wrong side)

(3) Cut to ¼"

Inner collar (right side)

(4)

Outer collar (wrong side)

7. Add gathers to the sleeves, and attach them to the shirt.

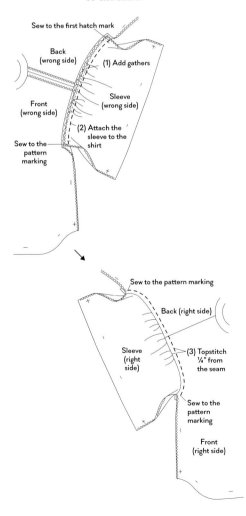

Sew to the first hatch mark

Back (wrong side)

(1) Add gathers

Front (wrong side)

Sleeve (wrong side)

Sew to the pattern marking

(2) Attach the sleeve to the shirt

Sew to the pattern marking

Back (right side)

Sleeve (right side)

(3) Topstitch ¼" from the seam

Sew to the pattern marking

Front (right side)

8. Sew along the underarm sleeve and side seams.

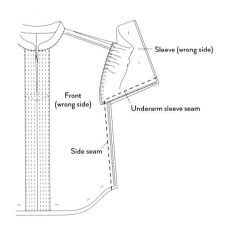

Sleeve (wrong side)

Front (wrong side)

Underarm sleeve seam

Side seam

Back view

Button-Back Tunic

Finished Measurements
(for sizes 4, 5, 6, and 7, respectively)

· Chest: 27½", 29⅛", 30¾", 32¼"
· Length: 19¼", 21", 22⅞", 24⅝"
· Sleeve length: 13¾", 15", 16½", 17¾"

Pattern Pieces: I from the Front of Sheet 1

· I Tunic front
· I Tunic back
· I Pocket
· I Collar
· I Sleeve

For the bias tape to finish the collar, cut according to
the measurements shown on the cutting layout.

Materials
(for sizes 4, 5, 6, and 7, respectively)

· Cotton fabric (44"–45" wide): 1¼ yards, 1¼ yards,
  1½ yards, 1½ yards
· Fusible interfacing: 36" x 23⅝", 23⅝", 27½",
  27½"
· Buttons: (5) ½" diameter

Preparation

· Apply fusible interfacing to the facing, the collar,
  and the folds of the pocket openings.
· Finish the seam allowances of the shoulders, sides,
  and underarms and the edges of the facing with a zigzag stitch (or overlock stitch).

Instructions
(★: Refer to diagram)

1. Fold the center-front tuck. (See page 62.) ★
2. Make the pockets, and attach them. (See page 41.)
3. Sew the shoulders, and press open the seam
   allowances. ★
4. Make the collar. ★
5. Attach the collar. Finish the seam allowance by
   wrapping it with the bias tape. ★
6. Attach the sleeves. Finish the seam allowances by
   binding the edges together with a zigzag stitch.
   (See page 41.)
7. Place the tunic front on the tunic back, right sides
   together, and sew from the opening edge of the
   sleeve to the bottom hem of the tunic. Press open
   the seam allowances. (See page 41.)
8. Fold the edge of the sleeve up by ⅜" and again by
   ¾" to create a double-fold hem, and stitch it in
   place.
9. Finish the hem. ★
10. Make buttonholes along the back edge, and attach
    the buttons. Make sure the buttonholes are
    vertical.

Cutting Layout (Size 5)

Add a seam allowance of ⅜"
unless otherwise specified.

denotes where to
apply interfacing

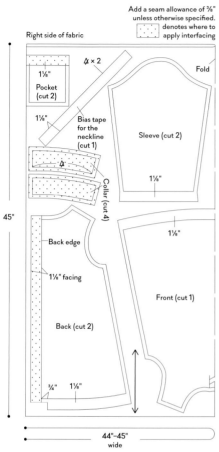

Right side of fabric

4 × 2

1⅛"
Pocket
(cut 2)

Fold

1⅛"

Bias tape
for the
neckline
(cut 1)

4

Collar (cut 4)

Sleeve (cut 2)

1⅛"

45"

Back edge

1⅛" facing

1⅛"

Front (cut 1)

Back (cut 2)

¾"   1⅛"

44"–45"
wide

Order of Instructions

Sizes and spacing
between buttons

4: 3⅜"
5: 3¾"
6: 4⅛"
7: 4½"

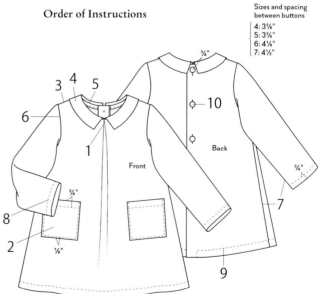

3 4 5

6

¾"

10

1

Front

Back

8

¾"

2

⅛"

¾"

7

9

1. Fold the center-front tuck.

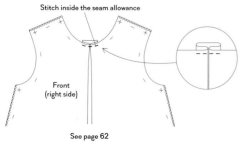

Stitch inside the seam allowance

Front
(right side)

See page 62

3. Sew the shoulder seams.

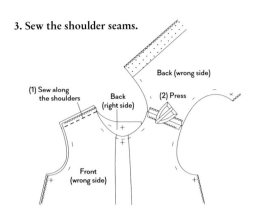

(1) Sew along the shoulders

Back (right side)

Back (wrong side)

(2) Press

Front (wrong side)

4. Make the collar.

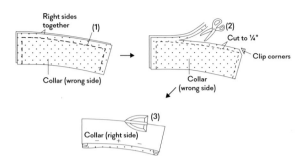

Right sides together

(1)

Collar (wrong side)

(2)

Cut to ¼"

Clip corners

Collar (wrong side)

(3)

Collar (right side)

5. Attach the collar.

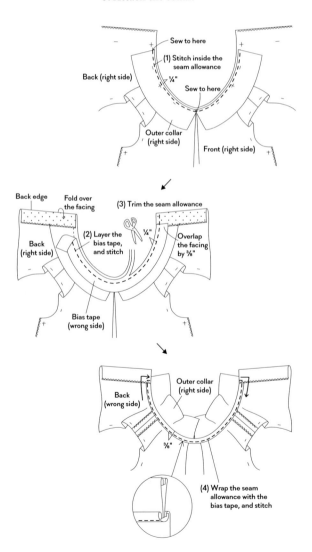

Sew to here

(1) Stitch inside the seam allowance

Back (right side)

¼"

Sew to here

Outer collar (right side)

Front (right side)

Back edge

Fold over the facing

(3) Trim the seam allowance

Back (right side)

(2) Layer the bias tape, and stitch

¼"

Overlap the facing by ⅜"

Bias tape (wrong side)

Back (wrong side)

Outer collar (right side)

⅜"

(4) Wrap the seam allowance with the bias tape, and stitch

9. Finish the hem.

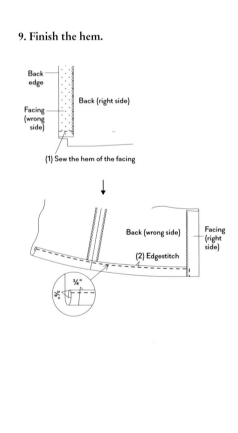

Back edge

Back (right side)

Facing (wrong side)

(1) Sew the hem of the facing

Back (wrong side)

Facing (right side)

(2) Edgestitch

¾"

⅜"

J

Photograph
on page 18

Collared Vest

Finished Measurements
(for sizes 4, 5, 6, and 7, respectively)

· Chest: 26¾", 28⅜", 30", 31½"
· Length: 12¼", 13", 13¾", 14½"

Pattern Pieces: J from the Front of Sheet 2

· J Vest front
· J Vest back
· J Welt pocket
· J Right belt trim
· J Left belt trim
For the front facing and the inner front vest, make
your own pattern by copying the outline of the front
vest, as shown on the cutting layout.

Materials
(for sizes 4, 5, 6, and 7)

· Napped linen fabric for vest (44"–45"): ¾ yard
· Linen fabric for lining (44"–45"): ½ yard
· Fusible interfacing: 36" x 15¾"
· Slide buckle: (1) ¾" wide
· Buttons: (3) ½" diameter

Preparation

· Apply fusible interfacing to the front vest where the
  pockets will attach, at the pocket openings, and on
  the facing.

Instructions
(★: Refer to diagram)

1. Make the pockets. (See page 41.)
2. Sew the center back seam of both the vest and the
   lining. Press open the seam allowances. (See page
   76.)
3. Make the belt and attach it. ★
4. Sew together the front lining and the facing, so
   that the seam allowances lie against the lining. ★
5. Sew together the side seams of vest and the lining,
   respectively, and press open the seam allowances.
6. Sew together the vest and the lining. Place them
   right sides together, and sew along the armholes
   and the back of the neckline. Then sew from the
   outside of the collar, down the front edge of the
   vest, and along the hem on both sides. Leave an
   opening along the back hem, then turn the vest
   right side out, and press it flat. Whipstitch the
   back opening, and topstitch along the outside
   of the collar, the front edge of the vest, and the
   hem. ★
7. Sew the shoulder seams. First, fold the front
   edges of the vest for the collar and secure them
   inside the seam allowance of the shoulder. Next,
   sew together the vest front shoulder and the vest
   back shoulder, being sure to leave the lining free.
   Then fold under the seam allowance of the lining
   back shoulder, and whipstitch it in place. ★
8. Stitch the armholes.
9. Make the buttonholes, and attach the buttons.

Cutting Layout (Size 5)

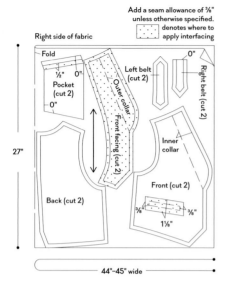

Add a seam allowance of ⅜"
unless otherwise specified.

[dotted box] denotes where to apply interfacing

Right side of fabric

Fold

½"   0"

Pocket (cut 2)

0"

0"

Left belt (cut 2)

Right belt (cut 2)

Outer collar

Front facing (cut 2)

Inner collar

Front (cut 2)

⅜"   1⅛"   ⅜"

Back (cut 2)

27"

44"–45" wide

Wrong side of fabric

Fold

Back (cut 2)

Front (cut 2)

18"

44"–45" wide

Order of Instructions

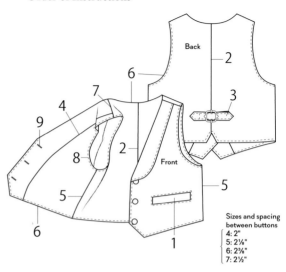

Back

2

6

3

7

4

9

8

2

Front

5

5

6

1

Sizes and spacing between buttons
4: 2"
5: 2⅛"
6: 2⅜"
7: 2½"

3. Make the belt, and attach it.

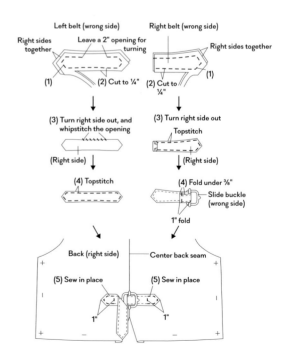

Left belt (wrong side)

Right sides together

Leave a 2" opening for turning

Right belt (wrong side)

Right sides together

(1)

(2) Cut to ¼"

(2) Cut to ¼"

(1)

(3) Turn right side out, and whipstitch the opening

(3) Turn right side out

Topstitch

(Right side)

(Right side)

(4) Topstitch

(4) Fold under ⅜"

Slide buckle (wrong side)

1" fold

Back (right side)

Center back seam

(5) Sew in place

(5) Sew in place

1"

1"

4. Sew together the front lining and the facing.

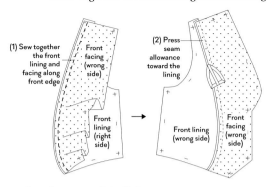

(1) Sew together the front lining and facing along front edge

Front facing (wrong side)

Front lining (right side)

(2) Press seam allowance toward the lining

Front lining (wrong side)

Front facing (wrong side)

6. Sew together the vest and the lining.

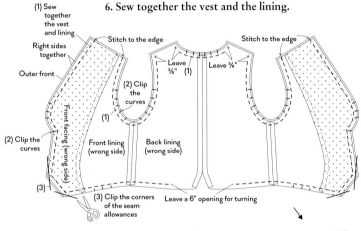

(1) Sew together the vest and lining

Right sides together

Outer front

Stitch to the edge

Leave ⅜" (1)

Leave ⅜"

Stitch to the edge

(2) Clip the curves

(1)

Front facing (wrong side)

Front lining (wrong side)

Back lining (wrong side)

(2) Clip the curves

(3)

(3) Clip the corners of the seam allowances

Leave a 6" opening for turning

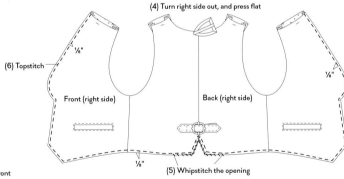

(4) Turn right side out, and press flat

(6) Topstitch

⅛"

Front (right side)

Back (right side)

⅛"

⅛"

(5) Whipstitch the opening

7. Sew the shoulder seams.

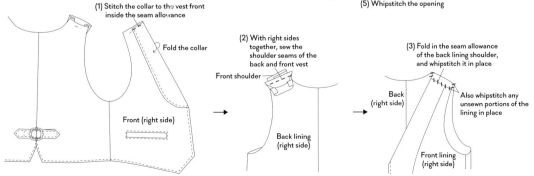

(1) Stitch the collar to the vest front inside the seam allowance

Fold the collar

Front (right side)

(2) With right sides together, sew the shoulder seams of the back and front vest

Front shoulder

Back lining (right side)

(3) Fold in the seam allowance of the back lining shoulder, and whipstitch it in place

Back (right side)

Also whipstitch any unsewn portions of the lining in place

Front lining (right side)

K

Photograph
on page 22

Suspender Pants

Finished Measurements
(for sizes 4, 5, 6, and 7, respectively)

- Hips: 28", 29⅛", 30⅜", 32¼"
- Length: 19⅝", 22⅜", 24⅞", 27⅛"

Pattern Pieces: K from the Front of Sheet 2

- K Pants front
- K Pants back
- K Waistband
- K Welt pocket
- K Facing
- K Placket
- K Left belt
- K Right belt
- K Front leather brace
- K Back leather brace

For enough material for 5 belt loops, cut according to the measurements shown on the cutting layout.

Materials
(for sizes 4, 5, 6, and 7, respectively)

For the Pants
- Linen fabric (58"–60" wide): 1 yard, 1 yard, 1 yard, 1¼ yards
- Fusible interfacing: 36" x 15¾"
- Zipper: 7⅞"
- Slide buckle: (1) ¾" wide
- Hook and bar closure: 1 set

For the Suspenders
- Elastic: 1" wide x 51" long
- Thin leather: 9⅞" x 6"
- Square rings: (2) 1" wide

- Metal adjusters: (2) 1" wide
- Buttons: (6) ½" diameter

Preparation

- Apply fusible interfacing to the waistband, the placket, the facing, the front of the pants where the pockets will attach, and the pocket openings.
- Finish the seam allowances of the rise, the edges of the placket and the facing, and the inner seam allowances of the welt pockets with a zigzag stitch (or overlock stitch).

Instructions
(★: Refer to diagram)

1. Make the pockets on the pants front. ★ (See page 41.)
2. Sew the front rise, and attach the zipper. ★
3. Sew the back rise, and press open the seam allowances.
4. Make the belt, and attach it to the pants back. (See page 68.)
5. Sew the sides using a flat-felled seam. ★
6. Sew the left and right inseams using a continuous flat-felled seam.
7. Create a double-fold hem by folding the fabric edge up by ½" and then again by 1", and stitch it in place.
8. Make the waistband. ★
9. Make the belt loops, and attach them. ★
10. Attach the hook and bar and the buttons.
11. Make the suspenders. ★

Cutting Layout (Size 5)

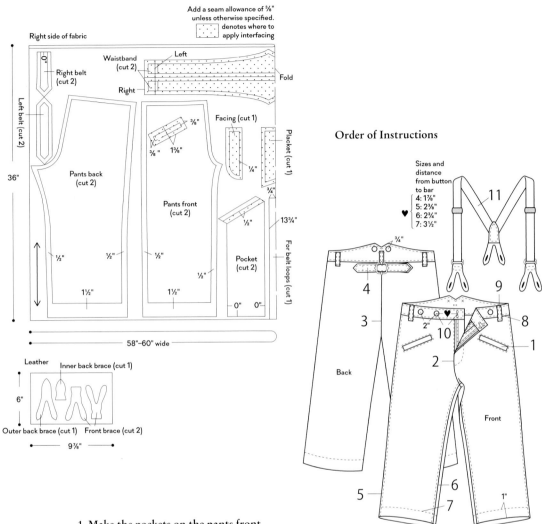

Add a seam allowance of ⅜" unless otherwise specified.

⋯ denotes where to apply interfacing

Right side of fabric

Waistband (cut 2)

Left

Right

Fold

Right belt (cut 2)

Left belt (cut 2)

36"

Pants back (cut 2)

⅜"

1⅜"

⅜"

Facing (cut 1)

¼"

Placket (cut 1)

¾"

Pants front (cut 2)

½"

13¾"

For belt loops (cut 1)

½"   ½"   ½"

½"

Pocket (cut 2)

½"

1½"   1½"   0"   0"

58"–60" wide

Leather

Inner back brace (cut 1)

6"

Outer back brace (cut 1)   Front brace (cut 2)

9⅞"

Order of Instructions

Sizes and distance from button to bar
4: 1⅞"
5: 2⅜"
6: 2¾"
7: 3½"

11

¾"

4

3

Back

2"

10

1

2

9

8

Front

5

6

7

1"

1. Make the pockets on the pants front.

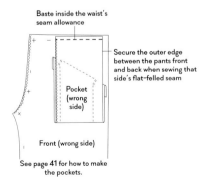

Baste inside the waist's seam allowance

Secure the outer edge between the pants front and back when sewing that side's flat-felled seam

Pocket (wrong side)

Front (wrong side)

See page 41 for how to make the pockets.

2. Sew the front rise, and attach the zipper.

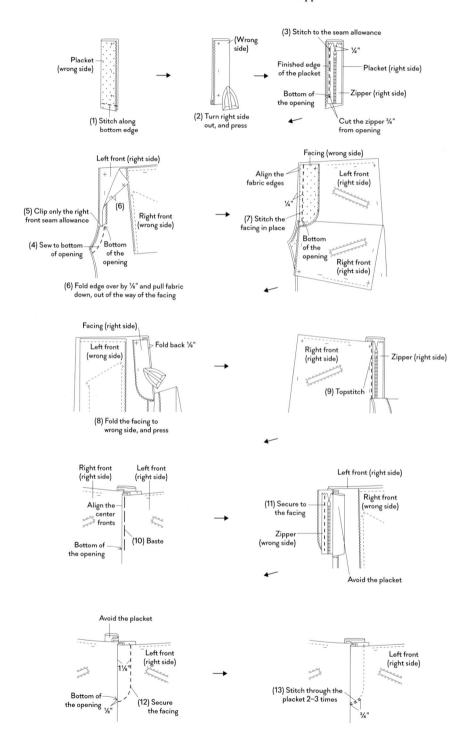

Placket (wrong side)

(1) Stitch along bottom edge

(Wrong side)

(2) Turn right side out, and press

(3) Stitch to the seam allowance

¼"

Finished edge of the placket

Placket (right side)

Bottom of the opening

Zipper (right side)

Cut the zipper ¾" from opening

Left front (right side)

(5) Clip only the right front seam allowance

(6)

Right front (wrong side)

(4) Sew to bottom of opening

Bottom of the opening

(6) Fold edge over by ⅛" and pull fabric down, out of the way of the facing

Facing (wrong side)

Align the fabric edges

Left front (right side)

¼"

(7) Stitch the facing in place

Bottom of the opening

Right front (right side)

Facing (right side)

Left front (wrong side)

Fold back ⅛"

(8) Fold the facing to wrong side, and press

Right front (right side)

Zipper (right side)

(9) Topstitch

Right front (right side)   Left front (right side)

Align the center fronts

Bottom of the opening

(10) Baste

Left front (right side)

(11) Secure to the facing

Right front (wrong side)

Zipper (wrong side)

Avoid the placket

Avoid the placket

Left front (right side)

1⅛"

Bottom of the opening   ⅛"

(12) Secure the facing

Left front (right side)

(13) Stitch through the placket 2–3 times

¾"

5. Sew the sides using a flat-felled seam.

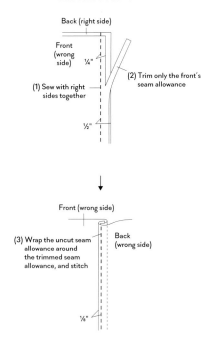

Back (right side)

Front (wrong side)

¼"

(2) Trim only the front's seam allowance

(1) Sew with right sides together

½"

Front (wrong side)

(3) Wrap the uncut seam allowance around the trimmed seam allowance, and stitch

Back (wrong side)

⅛"

8. Make the waistband.

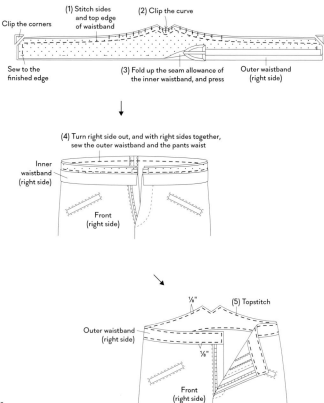

(1) Stitch sides and top edge of waistband

(2) Clip the curve

Clip the corners

Sew to the finished edge

(3) Fold up the seam allowance of the inner waistband, and press

Outer waistband (right side)

(4) Turn right side out, and with right sides together, sew the outer waistband and the pants waist

Inner waistband (right side)

Front (right side)

⅛"

(5) Topstitch

Outer waistband (right side)

⅛"

Front (right side)

9. Make the belt loops, and attach them.

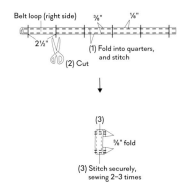

Belt loop (right side)

⅜"

⅛"

2½"

(1) Fold into quarters, and stitch

(2) Cut

(3)

⅜" fold

(3) Stitch securely, sewing 2–3 times

11. Make the suspenders.

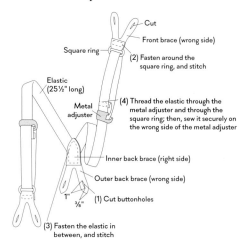

Cut

Front brace (wrong side)

Square ring

(2) Fasten around the square ring, and stitch

Elastic (25½" long)

Metal adjuster

(4) Thread the elastic through the metal adjuster and through the square ring; then, sew it securely on the wrong side of the metal adjuster

Inner back brace (right side)

Outer back brace (wrong side)

1"

⅜"

(1) Cut buttonholes

(3) Fasten the elastic in between, and stitch

L

Inside

Reversible Vest

Finished Measurements
(for sizes 4, 5, 6, and 7, respectively)

· Chest: 26¾", 28⅜", 30", 31½"
· Length: 12¼", 13", 13¾", 14½"

Pattern Pieces: L from the Front of Sheet 2

· L Vest front
· L Vest back
· L Welt pocket
· L Right belt
· L Left belt

Materials
(for sizes 4, 5, 6, and 7)

· Linen fabric for Fabric A (35"–36" wide): ¾ yard
· Striped linen fabric for Fabric B (58"–60" wide):
  ½ yard
· Fusible interfacing: 36" x 15¾"
· Slide buckle: (1) ¾" wide
· Buttons: (8) ½" diameter

Preparation

· On both Fabric A and Fabric B, apply fusible
  interfacing to the front edges of the vest, to where
  the pockets will attach, and to the pocket openings.

Instructions
(★: Refer to diagram)

1. Make the pockets for each of the front vests. ★
2. Sew the center back seam on each of the vests.
   Press open the seam allowances. ★
3. Make the belt, and attach it to each of the back
   vests. (See page 68.)
4. Sew the shoulder seams for each of the vests. Press
   open the seam allowances.
5. Sew the vests together. Place Vest A on Vest B,
   right sides together, and sew along the armholes,
   the back of the neckline, and from the front
   neckline to the front edge of the vest and the
   hem. Leave an opening along the back hem, and
   turn the vest right side out. Press flat, and
   whipstitch the opening. ★
6. Sew the shoulder seams. First, place the
   shoulders of Vest A right sides together, and sew;
   then, whipstitch the shoulders of Vest B. ★
7. Stitch the armholes and along the neckline to the
   front edge and the hem. ★
8. Make the buttonholes, and attach the buttons.
   Attach buttons to both sides of the vest.

Cutting Layout (Size 5)

Add a seam allowance of ⅜" unless otherwise specified.

⌜⋮⋮⌝ denotes where to apply interfacing

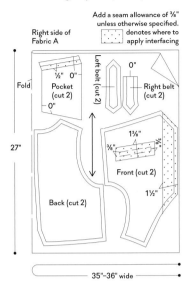

Right side of Fabric A

Fold

½" 0"
Pocket (cut 2)
0"

Left belt (cut 2)

0"
Right belt (cut 2)

1⅜"
⅜"
Front (cut 2)

1½"

Back (cut 2)

27"

35"–36" wide

Right side of Fabric B

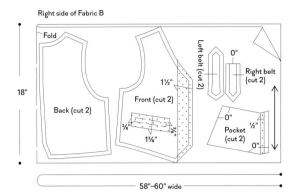

Fold

18"

Back (cut 2)

Left belt (cut 2)

1½"
Front (cut 2)
⅜"
1⅜"
⅜"

0"
Right belt (cut 2)

0"
½"
Pocket (cut 2)
0"

58"–60" wide

Order of Instructions

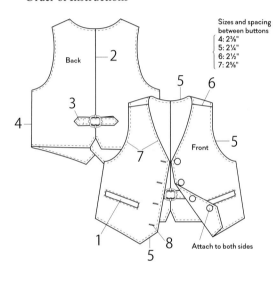

Back

2

3

4

5 6

7

Front

5

1

5 8

Attach to both sides

Sizes and spacing between buttons
4: 2⅜"
5: 2¼"
6: 2½"
7: 2⅝"

1. Make the welt pockets.

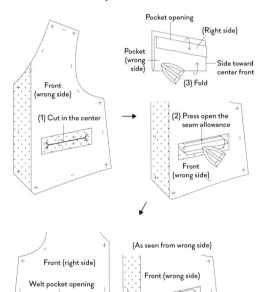

Front (wrong side)

(1) Cut in the center

Pocket opening

(Right side)

Pocket (wrong side)

Side toward center front

(3) Fold

(2) Press open the seam allowance

Front (wrong side)

Front (right side)

Welt pocket opening

1/16"

(4) Stitch the pocket to the vest front

Pocket (wrong side)

(As seen from wrong side)

Front (wrong side)

Finished fold

Pocket (right side)

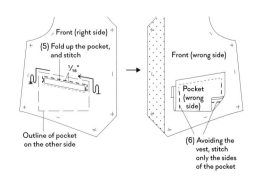

Front (right side)

(5) Fold up the pocket, and stitch

1/16"

Outline of pocket on the other side

Front (wrong side)

Pocket (wrong side)

(6) Avoiding the vest, stitch only the sides of the pocket

2. Sew the center back seam.

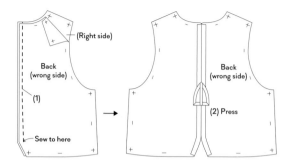

5. Sew the vests together.

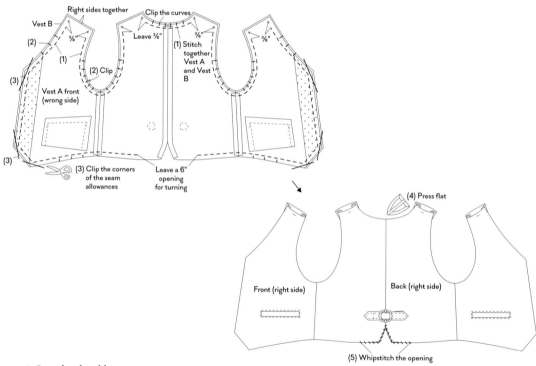

6. Sew the shoulder seams.

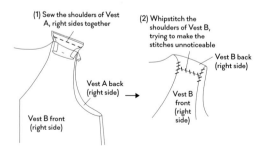

7. Topstitch the armholes and then along the neckline to the front edge and the hem.

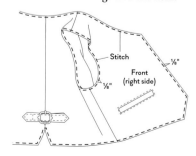

M

Photograph
on page 26

Hooded Poncho

Finished Measurements

(for sizes 4, 5, 6, and 7, respectively)

· Length: 14¾", 16⅛", 17½", 19"

Pattern Pieces: M from the Back of Sheet 2

· M Poncho front
· M Poncho back
· M Hood top
· M Hood side
· M Hood facing
· M Tab

For the bias tape to finish the neckline, cut according to the measurements shown on the cutting layout.

Materials

(for sizes 4, 5, 6, and 7, respectively)

· Linen Fabric (44"–45" wide): 1¼ yards, 1¼ yards, 1½ yards, 1¾ yards
· Fusible interfacing: 9⅞" x 27½"
· Buttons: (2) ¾" diameter
· Snaps: 4 sets

Preparation

· Apply fusible interfacing to the hood facing, the front facing on the poncho, and the tab.
· Finish the seam allowance of the edge of the front facing on the poncho with a zigzag stitch (or overlock stitch).

Instructions

(★: Refer to diagram)

1. Make the hood. (See page 99.)
2. Sew the shoulder seams. Finish the seam allowances by binding them together with a zigzag stitch that lies against the poncho back.
3. Attach the hood, and arrange the front edge of the poncho. ★
4. Create a double-fold hem by folding the edge up by ⅜" and then again by ½"; then, stitch along the hem, the front edge of the poncho, and the neckline.
5. Make the tab. ★
6. Attach the buttons and the snaps.

Cutting Layout (Size 5)

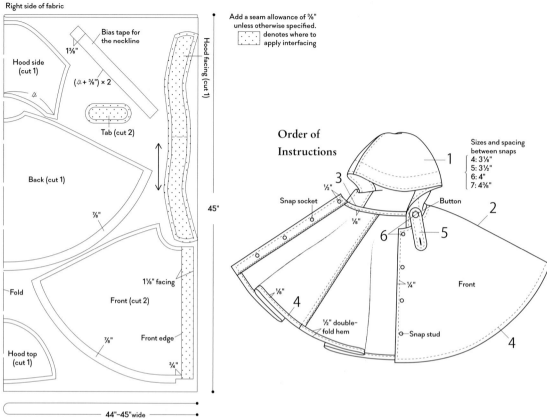

Right side of fabric

Bias tape for the neckline

1⅜"

Hood side (cut 1)

(△ + ⅜") × 2

Tab (cut 2)

Back (cut 1)

⅞"

Hood facing (cut 1)

45"

Fold

1⅛" facing

Front (cut 2)

Front edge

⅞"

Hood top (cut 1)

¾"

44"–45" wide

Add a seam allowance of ⅜" unless otherwise specified.

☐ denotes where to apply interfacing

Order of Instructions

1

Sizes and spacing between snaps
4: 3⅛"
5: 3½"
6: 4"
7: 4⅜"

3
½"

Snap socket

⅛"

Button

2

6

5

¼"

Front

½" double-fold hem

Snap stud

4

⅛"

4

3. Attach the hood, and arrange the front edge.

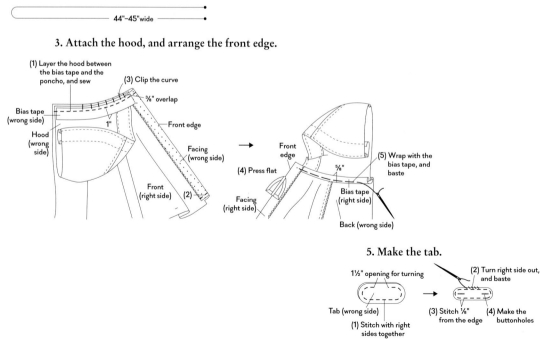

(1) Layer the hood between the bias tape and the poncho, and sew

(3) Clip the curve

⅜" overlap

Bias tape (wrong side)

1"

Hood (wrong side)

Front edge

Facing (wrong side)

Front (right side) (2)

(4) Press flat

Facing (right side)

Front edge

⅝"

(5) Wrap with the bias tape, and baste

Bias tape (right side)

Back (wrong side)

5. Make the tab.

1½" opening for turning

(2) Turn right side out, and baste

Tab (wrong side)

(1) Stitch with right sides together

(3) Stitch ⅛" from the edge

(4) Make the buttonholes

N

Photograph
on page 27

Yoke Panel Skirt

Finished Measurements
(for sizes 4, 5, 6, and 7, respectively)

• Waist: 21¼", 22", 22⅞", 24"
• Length: 12½", 13¾", 15", 16⅛"

Pattern Pieces: N from the Back of Sheet 2

• N Skirt front and back
• N Yoke front and back
For the left side opening placket, cut according to the measurements shown on the cutting layout.

Materials
(for sizes 4, 5, 6, and 7, respectively)

• Linen fabric (58"–60" wide): ¾ yard, ¾ yard,
  1 yard, 1 yard
• Fusible interfacing: 36" x 11⅞"
• Fabric-covered buttons: (4) ½" diameter

Preparation

Apply fusible interfacing to the yoke and the left side facing on the skirt front. Finish the seam allowance of the sides with a zigzag stitch (or overlock stitch).

Instructions
(★: Refer to diagram)

1. Sew the side seams of the skirt and the yoke, respectively. For the skirt, sew along the left side seam from the bottom of the opening. For the yoke, sew both the inner and outer yokes only on the right side. Press open each of the seam allowances.
2. Add gathers to the skirt, and sew on the outer yoke. When sewing the yoke on the front left side, fold the facing to the finished edge.
3. Make the placket, and attach it to the left side. ★
4. Attach the inner yoke. First, place the inner yoke on the outer yoke, right sides together, and sew along the left side and waist. For the left side back, fasten the placket between the inner and outer yokes, and sew. Next, turn the inner yoke right side out and baste the lower edge, folding in the seam allowance. Stitch along the waist. ★
5. Create a double-fold hem by folding up the edge by ⅜" and again by ¾"; then, stitch it in place.
6. Make the buttonholes on the left side front. Cover the buttons using the same fabric, and attach them to the placket.

Cutting Layout (Size 5)

Add a seam allowance of ⅜"
unless otherwise specified.

⋯ denotes where to
apply interfacing

Order of Instructions

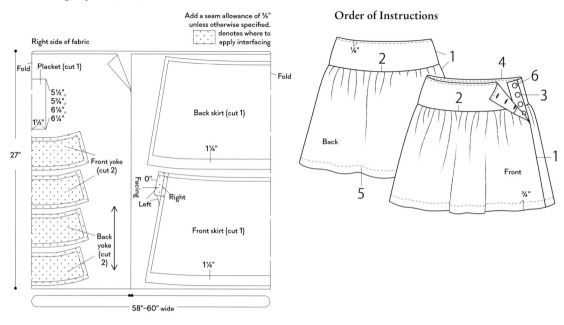

---

3. Make the placket, and attach it to the left side.

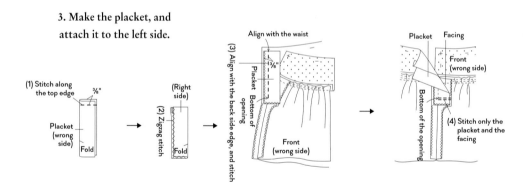

(1) Stitch along the top edge

Placket (wrong side)

Fold

⅜"

(2) Zigzag stitch

Fold

(Right side)

(3) Align with the back side edge, and stitch

Align with the waist

Placket

Bottom of opening

Bottom of opening

⅜"

Front (wrong side)

Placket

Facing

Front (wrong side)

Bottom of the opening

(4) Stitch only the placket and the facing

---

4. Attach the inner yoke.

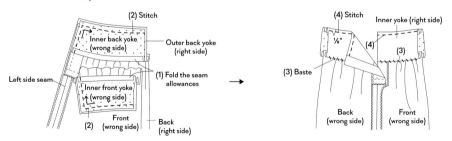

(2) Stitch

Inner back yoke (wrong side)

Outer back yoke (right side)

Left side seam

Inner front yoke (wrong side)

(1) Fold the seam allowances

Front (wrong side)

(2)

Back (right side)

(4) Stitch

Inner yoke (right side)

⅛"

(4)

(3)

(3) Baste

Back (wrong side)

Front (wrong side)

O

Photograph
on page 28

Coat Dress

Finished Measurements
(for sizes 4, 5, 6, and 7, respectively)

· Chest: 25¼", 26¾", 28⅜", 30"
· Length: 21⅞", 24", 26⅛", 28⅜"
· Sleeve length: 13¾", 15", 16½", 17¾"

Pattern Pieces: O from the Back of Sheet 1

· O Bodice front
· O Skirt front
· O Bodice back
· O Skirt back
· O Front facing
· O Sleeve
· O Pocket

For the back facing, make your own pattern by
copying the outline of the neckline of the bodice back,
as shown on the cutting layout.

Materials
(for sizes 4, 5, 6, and 7, respectively)

· Linen fabric (58"–60" wide): 1½ yards
· Fusible interfacing: 36" x 25½", 27½", 29½",
  31½"
· Buttons: (7) ½" diameter

Preparation

· Apply fusible interfacing to the front and back facing
  and to the seam allowances of the pocket openings on
  the skirt front.
· Finish the seam allowances of the shoulders, sides,
  and underarms, and the edges of the pockets, and the
  front and back facing with a zigzag stitch (or overlock
  stitch).

Instructions
(★: Refer to diagram)

1. Fold the pintucks on the skirt. ★
2. Sew together the bodice and the skirt. Finish the
   seam allowances by binding them together with a
   zigzag stitch that lies against the bodice.
3. Sew the shoulder seams of the bodice and the
   facing, respectively. Press open the seam
   allowances.
4. Place the facing on the bodice, right sides
   together, and sew all around the hem, the front
   edge, and the neckline of the facing. Clip the
   seam allowance of the neckline, turn the facing
   right side out, and press it flat.
5. Attach the sleeves. Finish the seam allowances by
   binding them together with a zigzag stitch. (See
   page 41.)
6. Sew along the underarm sleeves and the side
   seams, and make the pockets. (See page 41.)
7. Create a double-fold hem at the sleeve cuffs by
   folding the edge up by ⅜" and again by ¾", and
   stitch in place.
8. Create a double-fold hem at the bottom of the
   dress by folding the edge up by ⅜" and again by
   ¾", and stitch it in place. Topstitch along the
   front edge and the neckline.
9. Make the buttonholes, and attach the buttons.
   With the exception of the topmost buttonhole,
   make the buttonholes vertical.

Cutting Layout (Size 5)

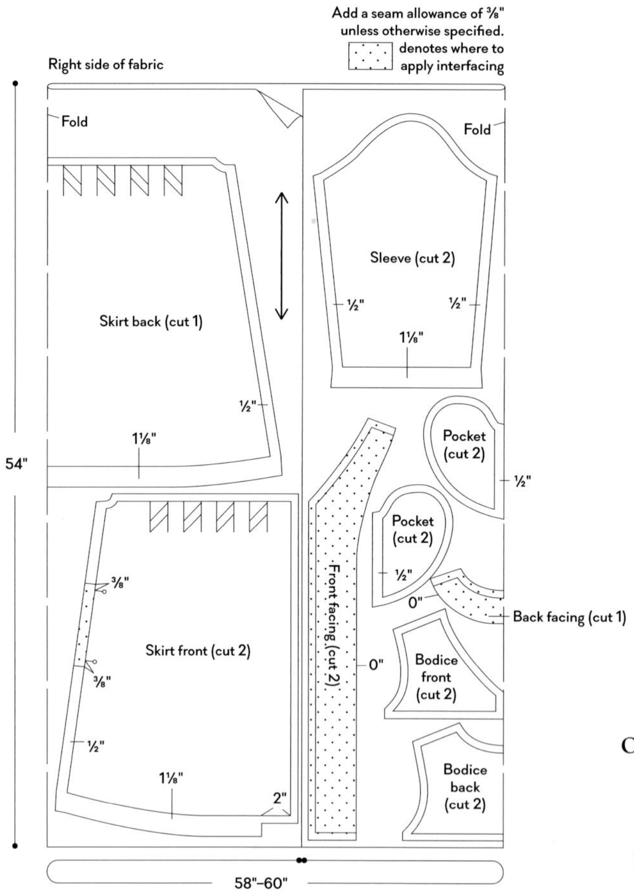

Add a seam allowance of ⅜" unless otherwise specified.
denotes where to apply interfacing
Right side of fabric
Fold
Fold
Skirt back (cut 1)
Sleeve (cut 2)
½"
½"
1⅛"
½"
1⅛"
54"
Pocket (cut 2)
½"
Pocket (cut 2)
½"
0"
Back facing (cut 1)
Front facing (cut 2)
0"
Bodice front (cut 2)
Skirt front (cut 2)
⅜"
⅜"
½"
1⅛"
2"
Bodice back (cut 2)
58"–60"

Order of Instructions

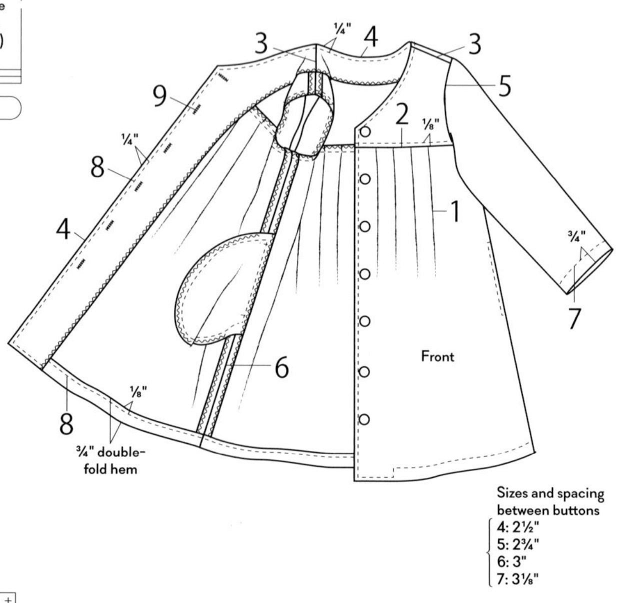

3
¼"
4
3
5
9
2
⅛"
¼"
8
1
4
¾"
7
Front
6
⅛"
8
¾" double-fold hem
Sizes and spacing between buttons
4: 2½"
5: 2¾"
6: 3"
7: 3⅛"

1. Fold the pintucks on the skirt.

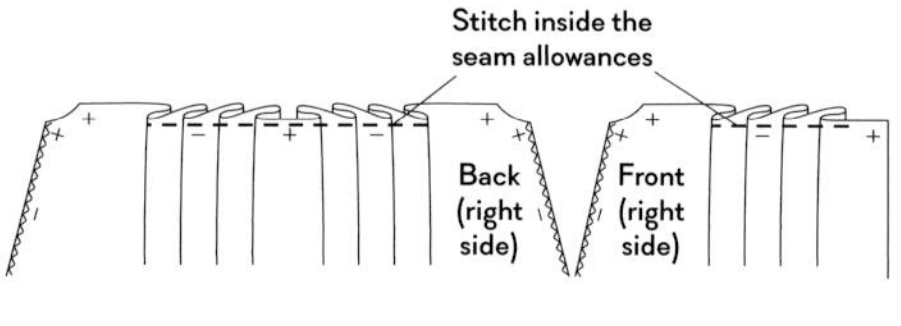

Stitch inside the seam allowances
Back (right side)
Front (right side)

P

Photograph
on page 29

Fleece Hat

Finished Measurements
(for sizes 4, 5, 6, and 7, respectively)

· Head circumference: 19", 19", 19¼", 19⅝"

Pattern Pieces: P from the Back of Sheet 2

· P Hat
For the string ties, cut according to the measurements
shown on the cutting layout.

Materials

· Fleece fabric (58"–60"): ½ yard
· Yarn: Worsted weight, as needed
· Thread suitable for sewing knit fabric

Notes

· Like a knit hat, this hat stretches when worn. Be sure
  to choose a fabric that gives, such as fleece.
· When sewing fabric that stretches, use machine
  thread suitable for knit fabric.

Instructions
(★: Refer to diagram)

1. Make the string ties, and baste them on. ★
2. Place two hat pieces right sides together, and sew
   along the outside. Make two—an outer hat and a
   lining—but for the lining, leave a 4" opening for
   turning. ★
3. Sew the lining and outer hat together. ★
4. Make a pompom with the yarn, and attach it. ★

Cutting Layout

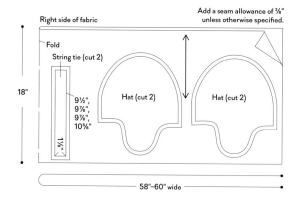

Right side of fabric

Fold

Add a seam allowance of ⅜" unless otherwise specified.

String tie (cut 2)

18"

9½",
9⅞",
9⅞",
10⅝"

1⅛"

Hat (cut 2)

Hat (cut 2)

58"–60" wide

Order of Instructions

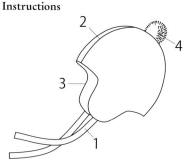

2

4

3

1

1. Make the string ties, and baste them on.

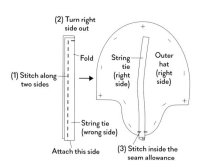

(2) Turn right side out

Fold

(1) Stitch along two sides

String tie (right side)

Outer hat (right side)

String tie (wrong side)

Attach this side

(3) Stitch inside the seam allowance

2. Place two hat pieces right sides together, and sew along the top edge.

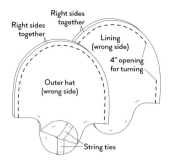

Right sides together

Right sides together

Lining (wrong side)

4" opening for turning

Outer hat (wrong side)

String ties

3. Sew the lining and outer hat together.

Lining (wrong side)

(3) Turn right side out through the opening

(4) Whipstitch the opening

(1) Stitch together

Lining (right side)

Press open the seam allowances

(2) Clip the curves

Outer hat (wrong side)

4. Make a pompom with the yarn, and attach it.

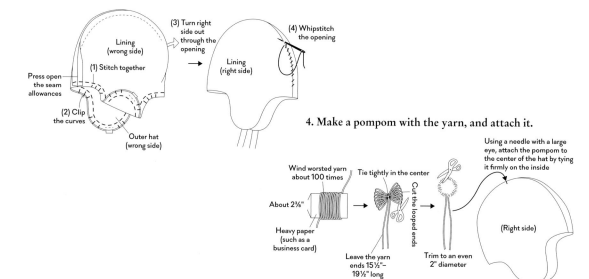

Wind worsted yarn about 100 times

Tie tightly in the center

Using a needle with a large eye, attach the pompom to the center of the hat by tying it firmly on the inside

About 2⅜"

Cut the looped ends

Heavy paper (such as a business card)

Leave the yarn ends 15½"–19½" long

Trim to an even 2" diameter

(Right side)

Q

Pullover Dress

Finished Measurements
(for sizes 4, 5, 6, and 7, respectively)

• Chest: 33", 35", 37", 39"
• Length: 23⅞", 26⅜", 28½", 31"
• Sleeve length: 12¼", 13⅜", 14¾", 16"

Pattern Pieces: Q from the Back of Sheet 1

• Q Dress front
• Q Yoke front
• Q Dress back
• Q Yoke back
• Q Collar
• Q Neckband
• Q Sleeve
• Q Cuff
• Q Trim
• Q Pocket

Materials
(for sizes 4, 5, 6, and 7, respectively)

• Linen fabric for dress (44"–45" wide): 2 yards,
  2 yards, 2¼ yards, 2¼ yards
• Cotton/linen fabric for yoke: 15¾" x 13¾"
• Fusible interfacing: 36" x 11⅞"
• Buttons: (4) ½" diameter; (3) ⅜" diameter

Preparation

• Apply fusible interfacing to the seam allowances of
  the front pocket openings, the facing on the front
  yoke, and the trim.
• Finish the seam allowances of the shoulders, sides,
  armholes, underarms, and sleeve caps, the edges of
  the pockets, and the edge of the yoke front's facing
  with a zigzag stitch (or overlock stitch).

Instructions
(★: Refer to diagram)

1. Fold the tucks on the dress front. ★
2. Sew together the yoke front and the dress front,
   and attach the trim. ★
3. Add gathers to the dress back. Place the yoke back
   on the dress back, right sides together, and sew.
   Finish the seam allowances by binding them
   together with a zigzag stitch that lies against the
   yoke edge.
4. Sew the shoulder seams, and press open the seam
   allowances.
5. Make the collar. ★
6. Attach the collar. ★
7. Add gathers to the sleeves, and attach them to the
   dress. ★
8. Sew the side and underarm sleeve seams, and
   make the pockets. ★
9. Add gathers to the sleeve edges, and attach the
   cuffs. ★
10. Create a double-fold hem by folding the edge by
    ⅜" and again by ¾", and stitch it in place.
11. Make the buttonholes, and attach the buttons.
    Make the buttonholes on the front edge vertical,
    and attach the ½" buttons. Make the buttonholes
    on the neckband and the cuffs horizontal, and
    attach the ⅜" buttons.

Cutting Layout (Size 5)

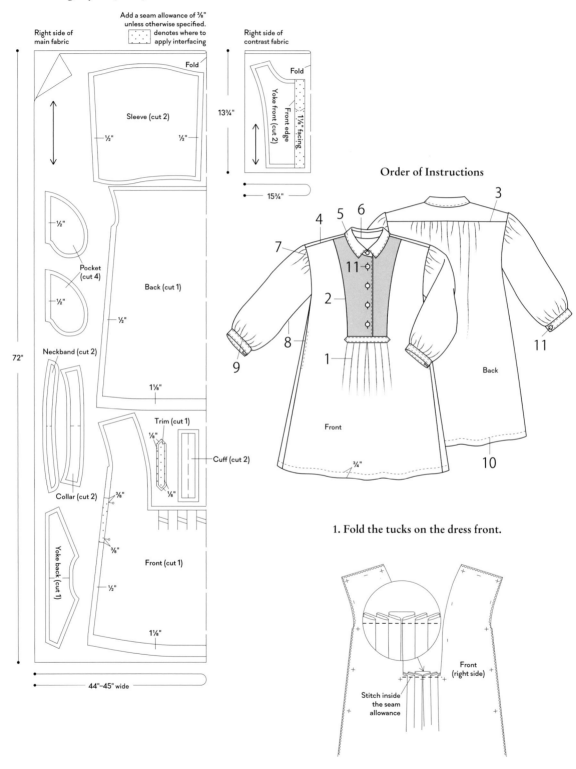

Add a seam allowance of ⅜"
unless otherwise specified.
∴ denotes where to
apply interfacing

Right side of
main fabric

Right side of
contrast fabric

Fold

Sleeve (cut 2)

½"   ½"

Pocket
(cut 4)

½"

½"

Back (cut 1)

½"

Neckband (cut 2)

1⅛"

Trim (cut 1)

⅛"

Cuff (cut 2)

Collar (cut 2)   ⅜"

⅜"

Yoke back (cut 1)

Front (cut 1)

½"

1⅛"

72"

44"–45" wide

Fold

Yoke front (cut 2)

Front edge

1¼" facing

13¾"

15¾"

Order of Instructions

3

4   5   6

7

11

2

8

1

9

Front

¾"

Back

11

10

1. Fold the tucks on the dress front.

Front
(right side)

Stitch inside
the seam
allowance

86

2. Sew together the yoke front and the dress front, and attach the trim.

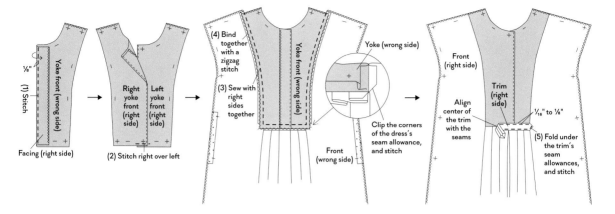

(1) Stitch

⅛"

Yoke front (wrong side)

Facing (right side)

Right yoke front (right side)

Left yoke front (right side)

(2) Stitch right over left

(4) Bind together with a zigzag stitch

(3) Sew with right sides together

Yoke front (wrong side)

Front (wrong side)

Yoke (wrong side)

Clip the corners of the dress's seam allowance, and stitch

Front (right side)

Align center of the trim with the seams

Trim (right side)

1/16" to ⅛"

(5) Fold under the trim's seam allowances, and stitch

5. Make the collar.

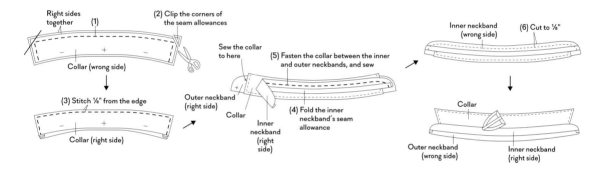

Right sides together

(1)

Collar (wrong side)

(2) Clip the corners of the seam allowances

(3) Stitch ⅛" from the edge

Collar (right side)

Sew the collar to here

Outer neckband (right side)

Collar

Inner neckband (right side)

(5) Fasten the collar between the inner and outer neckbands, and sew

(4) Fold the inner neckband's seam allowance

Inner neckband (wrong side)

(6) Cut to ⅛"

Collar

Outer neckband (wrong side)

Inner neckband (right side)

6. Attach the collar.

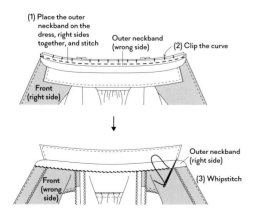

(1) Place the outer neckband on the dress, right sides together, and stitch

Outer neckband (wrong side)

(2) Clip the curve

Front (right side)

Outer neckband (right side)

Front (wrong side)

(3) Whipstitch

7. Add gathers to the sleeves, and attach them to the dress.

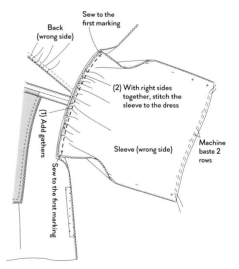

Back (wrong side)

Sew to the first marking

(2) With right sides together, stitch the sleeve to the dress

(1) Add gathers

Sew to the first marking

Sleeve (wrong side)

Machine baste 2 rows

8. Sew the side and underarm sleeve seams, and make the pockets.

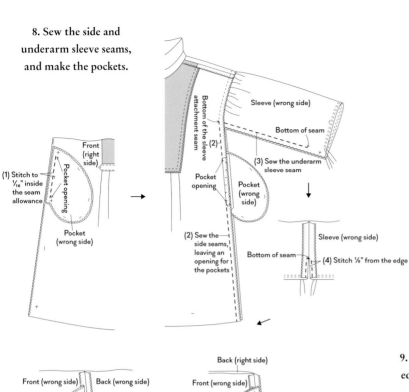

(1) Stitch to 1/16" inside the seam allowance

Front (right side)

Pocket opening

Pocket (wrong side)

Bottom of the sleeve attachment seam

(2)

Pocket opening

Pocket (wrong side)

(2) Sew the side seams, leaving an opening for the pockets

Sleeve (wrong side)

Bottom of seam

(3) Sew the underarm sleeve seam

Sleeve (wrong side)

Bottom of seam

(4) Stitch 1/8" from the edge

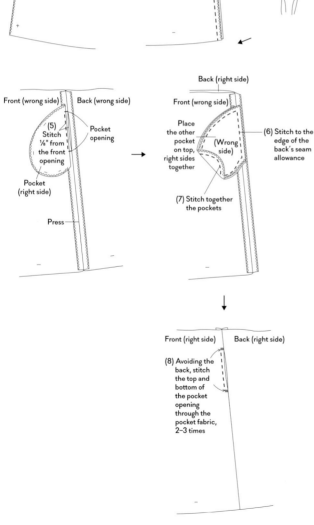

Front (wrong side)   Back (wrong side)

(5) Stitch 1/8" from the front opening

Pocket opening

Pocket (right side)

Press

Back (right side)

Front (wrong side)

Place the other pocket on top, right sides together

(Wrong side)

(6) Stitch to the edge of the back's seam allowance

(7) Stitch together the pockets

Front (right side)   Back (right side)

(8) Avoiding the back, stitch the top and bottom of the pocket opening through the pocket fabric, 2–3 times

9. Add gathers to the sleeve edges, and attach the cuffs.

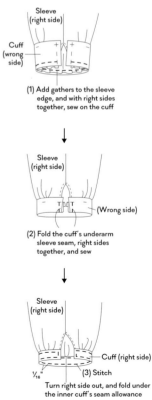

Sleeve (right side)

Cuff (wrong side)

(1) Add gathers to the sleeve edge, and with right sides together, sew on the cuff

Sleeve (right side)

(Wrong side)

(2) Fold the cuff's underarm sleeve seam, right sides together, and sew

Sleeve (right side)

Cuff (right side)

1/16"

(3) Stitch

Turn right side out, and fold under the inner cuff's seam allowance

R

Photograph
on page 31

Knickerbocker Puffed Pants

Finished Measurements
(for sizes 4, 5, 6, and 7, respectively)

· Waist: 21¼", 22", 22⅞", 24"
· Pant length: 12½", 13¾", 15⅛", 16½"

Pattern Pieces: R from the Back of Sheet 2

· R Pants front
· R Pants back
· R Yoke front and back
For the cuffs, cut according to the measurements
shown on the cutting layout.

Materials
(for sizes 4, 5, 6, and 7, respectively)

· Linen fabric (58"–60" wide): ¾ yard, ¾ yard,
  ¾ yard, 1 yard
· Fusible interfacing: 36" x 17¾"
· Zipper: 7⅞" long

Preparation

· Apply fusible interfacing to the yoke and the cuffs
  and to the seam allowance on the left side of the
  pants front where the zipper will be attached.
· Finish the seam allowances of the sides and inseams
  with a zigzag stitch (or overlock stitch).

Instructions
(★: Refer to diagram)

1. Fold the pleats in the pants. ★
2. Sew the rise on the pants front and back,
   respectively. Finish the seam allowances by
   binding them together with a zigzag stitch that lies
   against the left side of the pants.
3. Sew the right side seams on the pants and the
   inner and outer yokes, respectively. Press open
   the seam allowances.
4. Sew together the pants and the outer yoke. ★
5. Sew the left side seam, and attach the zipper. ★
6. Attach the inner yoke. Align the inner yoke along
   the waist of the outer yoke, right sides together,
   and sew. Turn the inner yoke right side out,
   whipstitch, then stitch at the waist. ★
7. Sew along the left and right inseams. Press open
   the seam allowances.
8. Add gathers to the hem, and attach the cuffs. ★

Cutting Layout (Size 5)

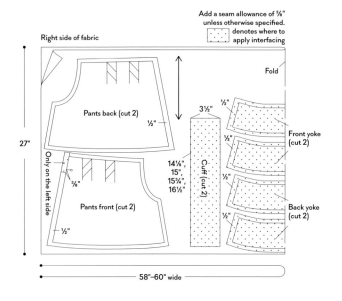

Add a seam allowance of ⅜"
unless otherwise specified.

[░] denotes where to
apply interfacing

Right side of fabric

Fold

27"

Pants back (cut 2)

½"

½"

3½"

½"

Front yoke
(cut 2)

½"

Cuff (cut 2)

14⅛",
15",
15¾",
16½"

½"

Only on the left side

⅜"

½"

Pants front (cut 2)

½"

Back yoke
(cut 2)

58"–60" wide

Order of Instructions

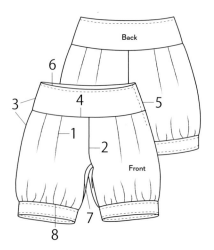

Back

6

3

4

5

1

2

Front

7

8

---

1. Fold the pleats in the pants.

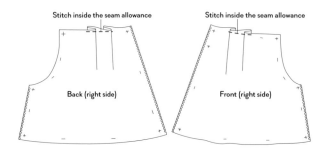

Stitch inside the seam allowance

Stitch inside the seam allowance

Back (right side)

Front (right side)

---

4. Sew together the pants and the outer yoke.

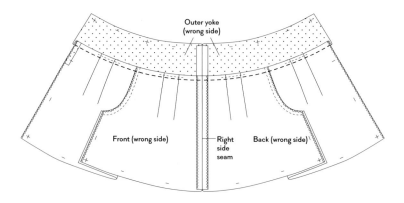

Outer yoke
(wrong side)

Front (wrong side)

Right
side
seam

Back (wrong side)

5. Sew the left side seam, and attach the zipper.

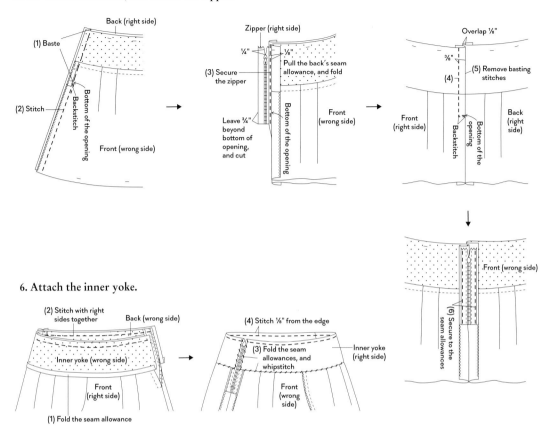

6. Attach the inner yoke.

(2) Stitch with right sides together

Back (wrong side)

(4) Stitch ⅛" from the edge

Inner yoke (wrong side)

Inner yoke (right side)

(3) Fold the seam allowances, and whipstitch

Front (right side)

Front (wrong side)

(1) Fold the seam allowance

8. Add gathers to the hem, and attach the cuffs.

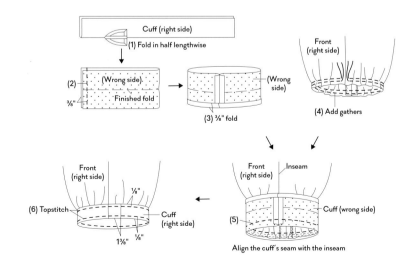

Cuff (right side)

(1) Fold in half lengthwise

(2)

(Wrong side)

Finished fold

⅜"

(Wrong side)

(3) ⅜" fold

Front (right side)

(4) Add gathers

Front (right side)

Inseam

Cuff (wrong side)

(5)

Align the cuff's seam with the inseam

Front (right side)

(6) Topstitch

⅛"

Cuff (right side)

1⅜" ⅛"

S

Photograph
on page 32

Elbow-Patch Jacket

Finished Measurements

(for sizes 4, 5, 6, and 7, respectively)

- Chest: 30", 31½", 33", 34⅝"
- Length: 14½", 15¾", 17", 18⅛"
- Sleeve length: 13¾", 15", 16½", 17¾"

Pattern Pieces: S from the Back of Sheet 2

- S Jacket front
- S Jacket back
- S Sleeve
- S Outer collar/Front facing
- S Inner collar
- S Back facing
- S Pocket
- S Elbow patch

For the belt, cut according to the measurements shown on the cutting layout.

Materials

(for sizes 4, 5, 6, and 7, respectively)

- Linen/wool fabric (58"–60" wide): 1 yard, 1 yard, 1¼ yard, 1¼ yard
- Linen fabric for contrast: 18" x 12"
- Fusible interfacing: 36" x 24"
- Buttons: (6) ¾" diameter

Preparation

- Apply fusible interfacing to the back facing, the outer collar/front facing, the inner collar, the belt, and the seam allowances of the pocket openings.
- Finish the seam allowances of the shoulders, sides, underarm sleeves, and edges of the front and back facing with a zigzag stitch (or overlock stitch).

Instructions

(★: Refer to diagram)

1. Make the pockets, and attach them. (See page 41.)
2. Attach the elbow patches to the sleeves. ★
3. Sew the shoulder seams, and press open the seam allowances.
4. Attach the inner collar to the jacket. ★
5. Attach the back facing to the outer collar/front facing. ★
6. Backstitch along the front edge and around the collar. ★
7. Sew the side seams, and press open the seam allowances.
8. Create a double-fold hem at the jacket edge by folding the fabric up by ⅜"and then again by ¾". Stitch along the hem, front edge, and around the collar. ★
9. Make the sleeves. Sew the underarm sleeve seams, and press open the seam allowances. Create double-fold hems at the cuffs by turning the edge of the sleeve up by ½" and again by ⅝", and stitch in place.
10. Attach the sleeves. Finish the seam allowances by binding them together with a zigzag stitch. (See page 41.)
11. Make the belt, and attach it. ★
12. Make the buttonholes, and attach the buttons.

Cutting Layout (Size 5)

Add a seam allowance of ⅜" unless otherwise specified.

[dotted pattern] denotes where to apply interfacing

Right side of fabric

Fold

Back facing (cut 1)

¼"

Outer collar (cut 1)

Sleeve (cut 2)

Belt (cut 2)

1⅜"

5⅙"

1⅛"

Front facing

¼"

Back (cut 1)

1⅛"

Pocket (cut 2)

1⅛"

Front (cut 2)

1⅛"

⅜"

36"

58"–60" wide

Contrast fabric

Inner collar (cut 1)

Elbow patch (cut 2)

12"

18"

Order of Instructions

Back

3

2

11

¾"   ¾"

12

6

8

5

4

10

7

Front

¾"

¼"

Sizes and spacing between buttons
4: 2⅜"
5: 2½"
6: 2¾"
7: 3"

9

½"

8

1

2. Attach the elbow patches to the sleeves.

⅛"

⅛"

Elbow patch (right side)

(1) Machine baste

Sleeve (right side)

(Right side)

(3) Stitch ⅛" from the edge

Insert a pattern made out of heavy paper

(Wrong side)

(2) Pull the threads, and fold the seam allowance

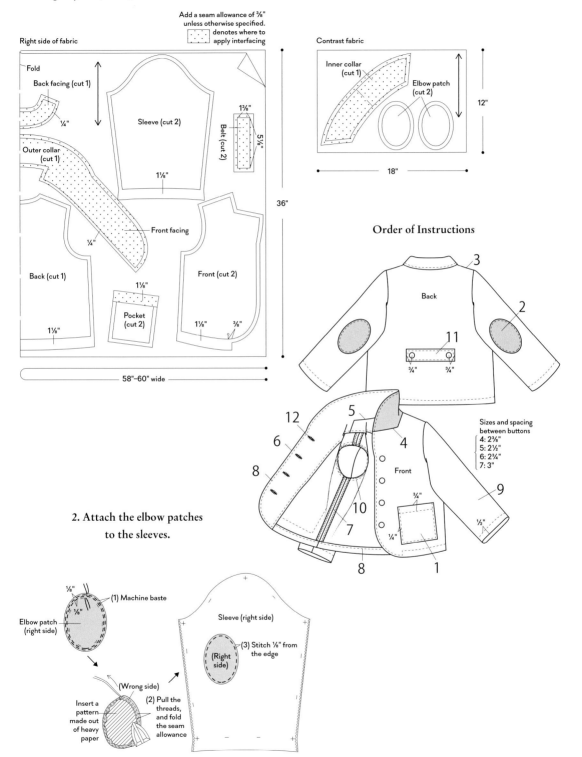

4. Attach the inner collar to the jacket.

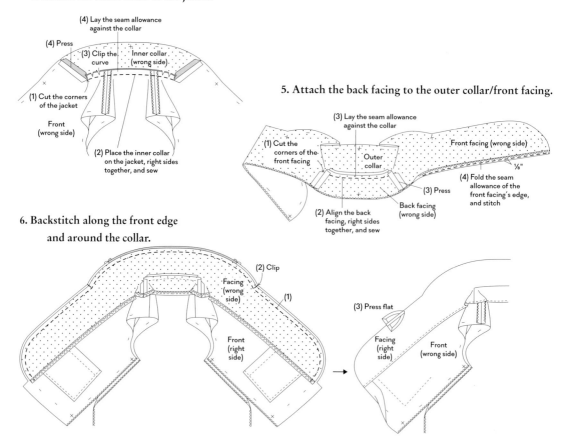

(4) Lay the seam allowance against the collar

(4) Press

(3) Clip the curve

Inner collar (wrong side)

(1) Cut the corners of the jacket

Front (wrong side)

(2) Place the inner collar on the jacket, right sides together, and sew

5. Attach the back facing to the outer collar/front facing.

(3) Lay the seam allowance against the collar

(1) Cut the corners of the front facing

Outer collar

Front facing (wrong side)

⅛"

(4) Fold the seam allowance of the front facing's edge, and stitch

(3) Press

Back facing (wrong side)

(2) Align the back facing, right sides together, and sew

6. Backstitch along the front edge and around the collar.

(2) Clip

Facing (wrong side)

(1)

Front (right side)

(3) Press flat

Facing (right side)

Front (wrong side)

8. Create a double-fold hem, and stitch along the hem, front edge, and around the collar.

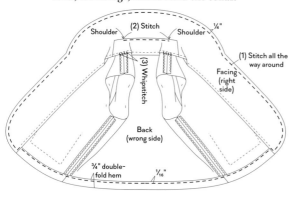

(2) Stitch

Shoulder

Shoulder

¼"

(3) Whipstitch

(1) Stitch all the way around

Facing (right side)

Back (wrong side)

¾" double-fold hem

¹⁄₁₆"

11. Make the belt, and attach it.

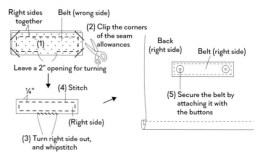

Right sides together

Belt (wrong side)

(2) Clip the corners of the seam allowances

(1)

Back (right side)

Belt (right side)

Leave a 2" opening for turning

¼"

(4) Stitch

(Right side)

(5) Secure the belt by attaching it with the buttons

(3) Turn right side out, and whipstitch

Photograph
on page 34

Back view

Sailor-Collar Pullover

Finished Measurements
(for sizes 4, 5, 6, and 7, respectively)

· Chest: 31½", 33", 34⅝", 36¼"
· Length: 17⅜", 19", 20½", 22"
· Sleeve length: 13¾", 15", 16½", 17¾"

Pattern Pieces: T from the Front of Sheet 1

· T Pullover front
· T Pullover back
· T Sleeve
· T Collar
· T Front facing
· T Pocket

For the back facing, make your own pattern by copying the outline of the neckline of the pullover back, as shown on the cutting layout.

Materials
(for sizes 4, 5, 6, and 7, respectively)

· Linen fabric: (58"–60" wide): 1 yard, 1¼ yard,
  1¼ yard, 1½ yard
· Fusible interfacing: 36" x 12"
· Buttons: (2) ½" diameter

Preparation

· Apply fusible interfacing to the front and back facing.
· Finish the seam allowances of the shoulders, sides, and underarm sleeves and the edges of the facing with a zigzag stitch (or overlock stitch).

Instructions
(★: Refer to diagram)

1. Sew the center-back tuck. ★
2. Make the pockets, and attach them. (See page 41.)
3. Sew the shoulder seams of the pullover and the facing, respectively, and press open the seam allowances.
4. Make the collar. ★
5. Attach the collar, and sew the front edge. ★
6. Fold the tuck on the pullover front. ★
7. Attach the sleeves. Finish the seam allowances by binding them together with a zigzag stitch that lies against the sleeve. (See page 41.)
8. Sew along the underarm sleeve and side seams. Press open the seam allowances. (See page 41.)
9. Create a double-fold hem at the jacket edge and cuffs by folding the fabric up by ⅜" and again by ¾", and stitch it in place.
10. Make the buttonholes, and attach the buttons.

Cutting Layout (Size 5)

Add a seam allowance of ⅜"
unless otherwise specified.
⬚ denotes where to
apply interfacing

Right side of fabric

Fold

0"

Back facing (cut 1)

Collar (cut 2)

Sleeve (cut 2)

1⅛"

Front facing (cut 2)

0"

Fold

45"

Back (cut 1)

1⅛"

Pocket
(cut 2)

1⅛"

Front (cut 1)

1⅛"

58"–60" wide

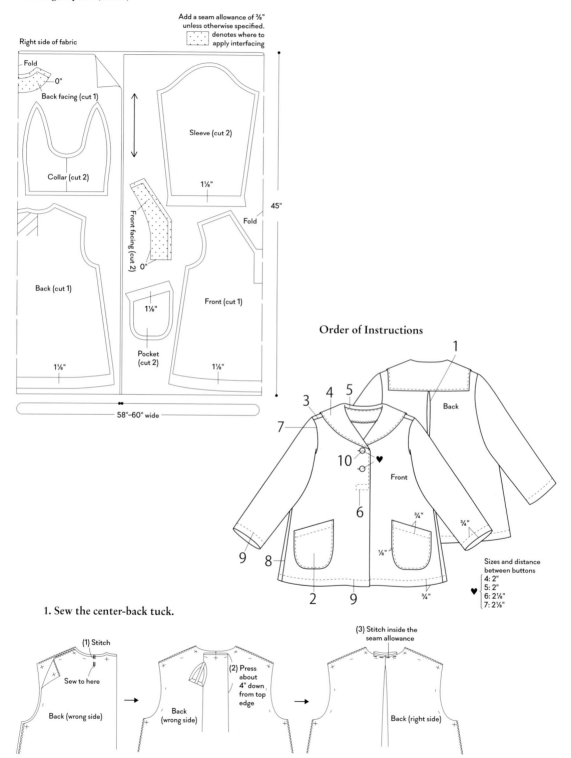

Order of Instructions

1

Back

3
4 5
7

10 ♥

Front

6

9 8

2 9

¾"

⅛"

¾"

¾"

Sizes and distance
between buttons
4: 2"
5: 2"
♥ 6: 2⅛"
7: 2⅛"

1. Sew the center-back tuck.

(1) Stitch

Sew to here

Back (wrong side)

(2) Press
about
4" down
from top
edge

Back
(wrong side)

(3) Stitch inside the
seam allowance

Back (right side)

4. Make the collar.

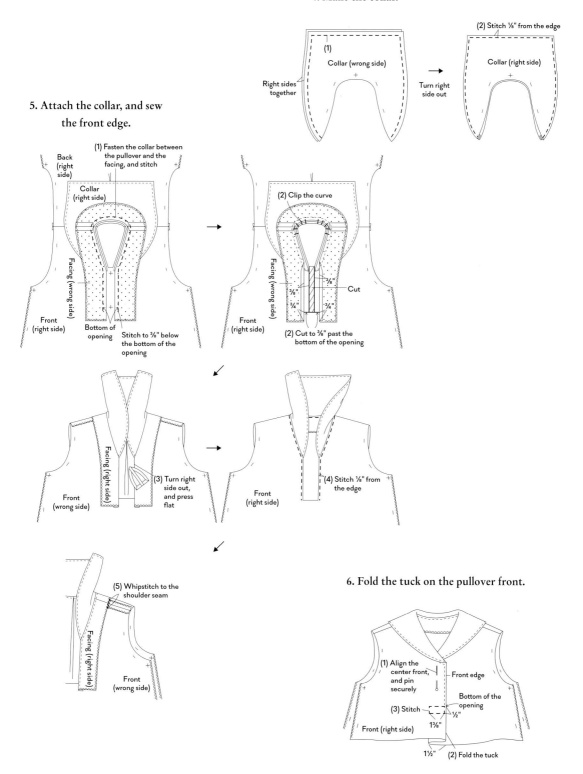

(1)

Collar (wrong side)

Right sides together

Turn right side out

(2) Stitch ⅛" from the edge

Collar (right side)

5. Attach the collar, and sew the front edge.

Back (right side)

(1) Fasten the collar between the pullover and the facing, and stitch

Collar (right side)

Facing (wrong side)

Front (right side)

Bottom of opening

Stitch to ⅜" below the bottom of the opening

(2) Clip the curve

Facing (wrong side)

Front (right side)

⅜"
⅜"
¾"
¾"

Cut

(2) Cut to ⅜" past the bottom of the opening

Facing (right side)

Front (wrong side)

(3) Turn right side out, and press flat

Front (right side)

(4) Stitch ⅛" from the edge

Facing (right side)

(5) Whipstitch to the shoulder seam

Front (wrong side)

6. Fold the tuck on the pullover front.

(1) Align the center front, and pin securely

Front edge

(3) Stitch

Bottom of the opening

½"

1⅜"

Front (right side)

1½"

(2) Fold the tuck

U

Photograph
on page 36

Hooded Scarf

Finished Measurements
(for sizes 4, 5, 6, and 7, respectively)

· Width: 6⅛", 6¼", 6½", 6⅝"
· Length: 53½", 55⅛", 56⅝", 58¼"

Pattern Pieces: U from the Back of Sheet 2

· U Hood top
· U Hood side
· U Hood facing
For the scarf, cut according to the measurements
shown on the cutting layout.

Materials
(for sizes 4, 5, 6, and 7, respectively)

· Linen/wool fabric: 31½" x 60", 31½" x 60",
  33½" x 60", 35½" x 63"
· Fusible interfacing: 6" x 27½"

Preparation

· Apply fusible interfacing to the hood facing.

Instructions
(★: Refer to diagram)

1. Make the hood. ★
2. Fold the scarf in half lengthwise, right sides
   together and fastening the hood between the scarf
   edges, and sew. ★
3. Turn right side out and press flat, whipstitch the
   opening, and stitch all the way around the
   outside.

Cutting Layout

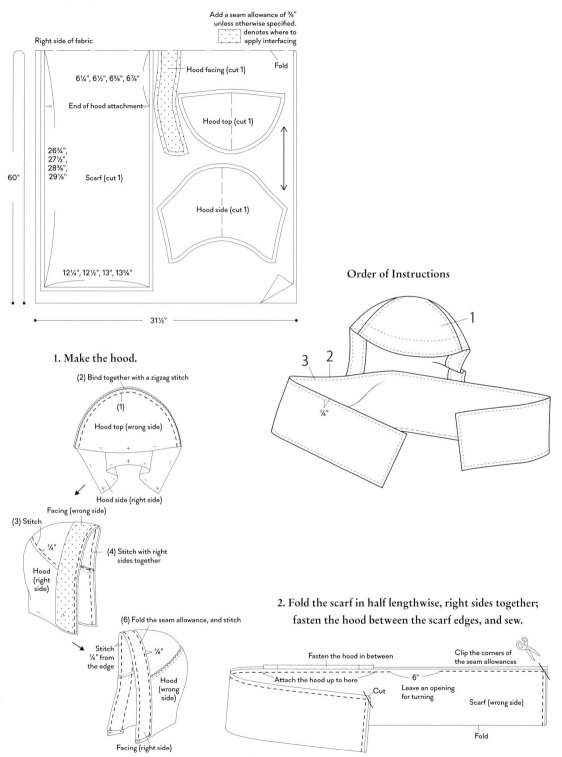

Add a seam allowance of ⅜" unless otherwise specified.

[dotted box] denotes where to apply interfacing

Right side of fabric

Fold

6¼", 6½", 6⅝", 6⅞"

End of hood attachment

Hood facing (cut 1)

Hood top (cut 1)

26¾",
27½",
28⅜",
29⅛"

Scarf (cut 1)

Hood side (cut 1)

60"

12¼", 12½", 13", 13⅜"

31½"

Order of Instructions

1

2

3

¼"

1. Make the hood.

(2) Bind together with a zigzag stitch

(1)

Hood top (wrong side)

Hood side (right side)

Facing (wrong side)

(3) Stitch

¼"

Hood
(right
side)

(4) Stitch with right sides together

(6) Fold the seam allowance, and stitch

Stitch
¼" from
the edge

⅛"

Hood
(wrong
side)

Facing (right side)

2. Fold the scarf in half lengthwise, right sides together; fasten the hood between the scarf edges, and sew.

Fasten the hood in between

Attach the hood up to here

Cut

6"

Leave an opening
for turning

Clip the corners of
the seam allowances

Scarf (wrong side)

Fold

Akiko Mano

Born into a family of dressmakers, Akiko Mano learned sewing from a young age. After becoming a mother, she began making children's clothes and studied pattern making at Bunka Fashion College. Her children's clothing, made of natural materials and styled to look like grown-ups', has garnered a great deal of attention. She is also the author of *Linen, Wool, Cotton*. www.sea.sannet.ne.jp/jamjam/

Roost Books
An imprint Shambhala Publications, Inc.
Horticultural Hall
300 Massachusetts Avenue
Boston, Massachusetts 02115
roostbooks.com

© 2010 by Akiko Mano
Originally published as *Oshare ga suki na onna no ko no fuku* by Akiko Mano in Japan in 2010
by EDUCATIONAL FOUNDATION BUNKA GAKUEN BUNKA PUBLISHING BUREAU, Tokyo.
World English translation rights arranged with EDUCATIONAL FOUNDATION BUNKA GAKUEN
BUNKA PUBLISHING BUREAU through The English Agency (Japan) Ltd.
Translation © 2014 by Shambhala Publications, Inc.
Translation by Allison Markin Powell
Bunka Staff Credits
Book design: Knoma
Photography: Yoshiharu Koizumi
Stylist: Rieko Ohashi
Hair & Makeup: Atsushi Momiyama (BARBER 410)
Models: Rosa, Maya, Abby, Ellie, Yoko, Alicia
Technical editor: Naoko Domeki
Digital tracing: Miki Masui
Pattern grading: Kazuhiro Ueno
Editor: Kaori Tanaka (BUNKA PUBLISHING BUREAU)
Publisher: Sunao Onuma

9 8 7 6 5 4 3 2 1

First English Edition
Printed in China

∞ This edition is printed on acid-free paper that meets the
American National Standards Institute z39.48 Standard.
♻ Shambhala Publications makes every effort to print on recycled paper.
For more information please visit www.shambhala.com.
Distributed in the United States by Penguin Random House LLC
and in Canada by Random House of Canada Ltd

Library of Congress Cataloging-in-Publication Data
Mano, Akiko. [Oshare ga suki na onna no ko no fuku. English]
Linen, wool, cotton kids: 21 patterns for simple separates and comfortable layers / Akiko Mano.
Pages   cm
isbn 978-1-61180-158-3 (pbk.: alk. paper)
1. Children's clothing—Pattern design. 2. Machine sewing. I. Title.
TT640.M2813 2014
646.4'06—dc23
2013033312